THE GROUND WE SHARE

THE GROUND WE SHARE

Everyday Practice, Buddhist and Christian

Robert Aitken
David Steindl-Rast

EDITED BY
NELSON FOSTER

SHAMBHALA
Boston & London
1996

Shambhala Publications, Inc.
Horticultural Hall
300 Massachusetts Avenue
Boston, Massachusetts 02115

9 8 7 6 5 4 3 2 1

First Shambhala Edition
Printed in the United States of America
♾ This edition is printed on acid-free paper that meets the
American National Standards Institute Z39.48 Standard.
Distributed in the United States by Random House, Inc.,
and in Canada by Random House of Canada Ltd

Library of Congress Cataloging-in-Publication Data
Aitken, Robert, 1917–
The ground we share: everyday practice, Buddhist and Christian/
Robert Aitken, David Steindl-Rast; edited by Nelson Foster.
p.   cm.
Originally published: Liquori, Mo.: Triumph Books, © 1994.
Includes bibliographical references and index.
ISBN 1-57062-219-1 (alk. paper)
1. Spiritual life—Comparative studies. 2. Christianity and other
religions—Buddhism. 3. Buddhism—Relations—Christianity.
I. Steindl-Rast, David. II. Foster, Nelson. III. Title.
BL624.A38   1996   95-51654
261.2'43—dc20   CIP

CONTENTS

PART THREE

Practicing in Institutions,
Practicing in Society

Editor's Introduction

ARCING SOUTH AND EAST from the northern tip of the island of Hawai'i, the Kohala Mountains form a crescent that captures moisture-laden clouds blowing in off the Pacific and traps the resulting rain in a succession of hidden valleys. The largest and southernmost of these valleys is Waipi'o, whose name means "curving water" and whose lush bottomlands have been cultivated by Hawaiians for hundreds of years. A four-thousand-foot *pali,* or cliff, separates Waipi'o from the nearest paved road, and though its broad basin once supported a large Hawaiian population, now it is home to only sixty people, mainly farming families. An anomaly in a land where tourism prevails, it has no hotels and receives few overnight visitors other than local men going to hunt feral pigs in the even more isolated valleys beyond.

The two elders who entered the valley one bright day in January 1991, were uncommon visitors—but they would be uncommon visitors almost anywhere, any time. Zen master Robert Aitken and Benedictine brother David Steindl-Rast retired to Waipi'o to live together for a week and especially to talk, to consult one another. It was to be a private conversation between old friends, thus exceptionally searching and frank, but from the outset, they imagined it, too, as a dialogue for others, its fruits to be offered through publication. This book fulfills that hope, giving all who wish it a chance to join these eminent teachers in the silence of Waipi'o and to listen in as they speak about what matters most to them and matters most, perhaps, to the future of our society and world: a deep and abiding practice of religious life.

The two men traveled very different routes to their retreat in Waipi'o. Aitken Rōshi is a lifelong resident of Hawai'i, having moved to Honolulu with his family at the age of five. Born in 1917, he was raised in the Protestant church and still peppers his presentations with biblical passages he absorbed in the pews of his boyhood and at his grandparents' dinner tables. As a young man, however, he was more inclined to poetry than to religion and more to playing cards than to attending his classes at the University of Hawaii. In 1941, having flunked out of the university and feeling none of the war fever that was stirring his family and community, he contrived to leave Honolulu by taking a clerical job on the island of Guam. Being captured there in the week following the Pearl Harbor attack was the turning point of his life, leading to a four-year internment in Japan, a lifelong commitment to pacifism, and a strangely seren- dipitous exposure to Zen, first through the book *Zen in English Literature and Oriental Classics* and later through a consolidation of internment camps that united him with its author, R. H. Blyth.

Over the next three decades, Bob Aitken doggedly pursued Zen study while getting on with lay life. He took both a bache- lor's degree in English literature and a master's in Asian litera- ture at the University of Hawaii, married and fathered a son, divorced and later remarried, worked in various capacities— community organizer, bookshop clerk, English teacher, admin- istrator at the East-West Center in Honolulu. Moving back and forth from Hawai'i to California and Japan, he was able to train with four Japanese Zen masters, each of whom is recognized today as a formative figure in Western Zen: Nyogen Senzaki, Nakagawa Sōen Rōshi, Yasutani Hakuun Rōshi, and Yamada Kōun Rōshi. He completed the formal course of study under Yamada Rōshi, abbot of a lay Japanese lineage known as the Sanbō Kyodan, and in 1974 received his authorization to teach Zen as an independent master.

Fifteen years earlier, he and his second wife, Anne Hopkins Aitken, had established a Zen Buddhist society named the Diamond Sangha, and through their unstinting efforts, it had grown by this time into a thriving, if somewhat ragtag, organization with temples on the islands of Maui and Kaua'i as well as in Honolulu. Receiving fresh impetus with Aitken Rōshi's designation as one of the first Western Zen masters, in the ensuing decades the Diamond Sangha has further expanded and now constitutes a network of groups dotted about the United States, South America, and Australia.

Many students have been attracted through the string of books Aitken Rōshi has published since 1978, books noteworthy for combining clear and enthusiastic instruction in Zen with profound ethical and political concerns. The latter concerns distinguish not only his literary productions but his entire adult life. In his effort to live out the implications of Buddhist practice, he joined in founding the Hawai'i branch of the American Civil Liberties Union, served as a draft counselor during the Vietnam War, campaigned against that war and every subsequent U.S. military intervention, took part in nonviolent civil disobedience to protest weapons of mass destruction, and became a dedicated advocate for human rights and deep ecology. He continues to rally fellow Buddhists to engage in social issues, both by his example and as a co-founder and guiding light of the Buddhist Peace Fellowship.

His personal rectitude and activism have endeared Aitken

Rōshi to Buddhists throughout the United States, and his still-growing stature led Helen Tworkov, the author of *Zen in America*, to dub him "the unofficial American dean of Zen." With the translation of his books into Spanish, German, and several other languages has come international recognition as a pivotal figure in the establishment of an authentic Zen tradition in the West.

Like Yamada Rōshi before him, Aitken Rōshi has urged interested Christians to study Zen without forsaking their own traditions and has had many Christians, both lay and ordained, among his students. Roman Catholics have proven especially receptive to Zen practice and have come to play an increasingly prominent part in both the Sanbō Kyodan and the Diamond Sangha. Of the four students Aitken Rōshi has authorized to teach as independent Zen masters, one is a Catholic priest— Patrick Hawk of the Redemptorist order—and a Catholic sister is among those now serving apprenticeships as Diamond Sangha teachers. Such appointments take some people aback but really represent nothing more than a new wrinkle in a twenty-five-century tradition of Buddhist accommodation to, and integration of, other religions.

In several senses, the journey to Waipi'o was longer for Brother David than for Aitken Rōshi. Not only had he flown three thousand miles across the Pacific from the Big Sur hermitage where he spends most of his time, but he had also traveled a vast distance, in the course of his lifetime, from his birthplace in the Old World and from his church's once-categorical rejection of other religious ways. He describes himself as a bridge-builder, and so he is, but building a bridge often requires blazing a route, and he has displayed abundant readiness, if not eagerness, to jump intellectual and social chasms and venture toward new frontiers.

Nine years junior to Aitken Rōshi, Brother David is a native of Austria, and the tones of his mother tongue, German, still play in his excellent English. Born in Vienna, he moved with his mother and two younger brothers to a village in the Austrian Alps, when his parents' marriage dissolved. In its two-room school, close-knit community, and encompassing mountains, he received an education very rich in culture and nature. A large part of village life revolved around the Catholic church and its celebrations, and throughout the explorations of his adulthood, he has always steered his course by the constellation of faith, rite, and experience he came to know in those early years.

Like his dialogue partner, Brother David was deeply affected by the Second World War. He was twelve, attending a progressive church boarding school in the capital, when Nazi storm troopers took Austria in 1938. As older schoolmates were conscripted and began to die in the armies of the Third Reich, David and his friends engaged in symbolic acts of resistance and found in their faith an ever-more-needed source of direction and strength. He himself was forced into the German ranks in 1944 but escaped after a year and lived underground until war's end permitted him to return to his schooling. An undergraduate degree in painting at the Vienna Academy of Fine Arts led to work as a restorer of art damaged in the war, but then he went on, inspired by parallels between the artwork of children and indigenous peoples, to earn a doctorate in psychology (with a minor in anthropology) at the University of Vienna.

Dr. Steindl-Rast unexpectedly became Brother David in 1953, the year after completing his Ph.D. His mother, grandmother, and brothers by then had emigrated to the United States, and while visiting them, he learned that a group of Benedictine monks were forming a community near Elmira, in the Finger Lake region of New York, to revive the original vision of monastic life propounded in the sixth century by the founder of their order. The Rule of Saint Benedict had strongly appealed to him when he was first introduced to it in the wake of the war, and he leapt at this chance to join in practicing the regimen that it prescribed: humility, manual labor, prayer, study, and life in community. For the following twelve years, he immersed himself in this discipline, rarely leaving the farm-cum-monastery.

The monks of Mount Saviour, though numbering not many more than a dozen, developed a reputation for the earnestness of their endeavor and the vitality of their intellectual life. Many of the brightest lights in U.S. Catholic circles came as visitors, attracted also by the good name of their prior, Father Damasus Winzen, a wise and inspiring guide and well-known scholar of liturgy and art. Brother David's studies, focusing on philosophy and theology, were informed by his own deep-seated social consciousness and by the work and writings of Daniel Berrigan, a frequent guest at the monastery, and of Dorothy Day, matriarch of the Catholic Worker movement. Ever since, within the parameters of his vocation as a monk, he has spoken out on war, poverty, and other social problems, taking a particular interest in addressing groups least likely, at first thought, to receive his message gladly—Green Berets, naval cadets at Annapolis, corporate executives.

In the mid-1960s, the openness to other religions expressed by the Second Vatican Council gave Brother David an opportunity to cultivate his interst in Zen Buddhism, an interest seeded by the books of D. T. Suzuki. He sought and received permission to study Zen and did so first with the young monk Tai Shimano, then with two teachers who figured prominently in Aitken Rōshi's training—Yasutani Rōshi and Sōen Rōshi—and later with Shunryū Suzuki Rōshi of San Francisco Zen Center. Independently, the great Trappist monk Thomas Merton had undertaken a parallel exploration of Buddhism, and when Father Damasus introduced the two in 1966, they became close friends and colleagues, agreeing that Buddhism furnished new keys to their own faith.

While Merton's investigations ended with his untimely death

in 1968, Brother David went on not only to deepen his Zen practice but also to acquaint himself with other wisdom traditions such as Sufism and to study points of intersection between the insights of religion and those of modern science. Though he remains a hermit at heart, he travels part of each year, sharing his discoveries as a lecturer and spiritual guide. He has published three prior books, including a book of conversations with Fritjof Capra and Thomas Matus titled *Belonging to the Universe: Explorations on the Frontier of Science & Spirituality.*

Aitken Rōshi and Brother David met in passing in 1968, but it was twelve years later, co-chairing a panel at the inaugural conference of the Society for Buddhist-Christian Studies in Honolulu, that their friendship was sealed. After several further meetings and a lively correspondence, they decided to undertake a book that would treat much the same themes discussed in the following pages. Other commitments and the difficulties of collaborating by mail soon reduced this project to an exchange of apologies, however, and they abandoned the idea until 1990, when Brother David, fresh from his conversations with Capra and Matus, suggested that they employ the same means—talk and tape recorder.

So it was that they found themselves clutching their seats and clenching their teeth as Waipiʻo resident Burt Arriens steered his Land Rover along the washed-out dirt road that descends the precipitous *pali* into the valley. The view unfolding before them reminded Brother David more of ancient Samoa than of modern Hawaiʻi. Rock-walled agricultural terraces built by Hawaiians of old are still planted largely in taro, the water-loving Polynesian staple, and the head of the valley is heavily forested. On reaching the valley floor, Arriens turned away from the sea, following a meandering track through the taro paddies toward their destination deep on the opposite side of the valley. Six times the route crossed the tributaries or main channel of Wailoa Stream, and his passengers held their breath as Arriens pitched the Land Rover down one bank and gunned it up a seemingly impossible grade on the other. Well before arriving, Aitken Rōshi remembers, they passed a sign warning: NO MOTOR TRAFFIC BEYOND THIS POINT.

The road led into the rain forest, and Arriens eventually deposited his riders at a cabin surrounded and overhung by lanky, silvery-leaved kukui trees. Aitken Rōshi had arranged to rent this rustic dwelling from a college friend, who built it as a family retreat twenty years ago and now sometimes lets it to vacationers seeking a getaway far from Waikiki's amenities or crowds. For the week of their conversation, the two men would have no electricity, no flush toilet, no phone, no news, and no visitors except Burt Arriens, dropping in periodically to replenish their supplies. The only other person they would encounter was Brother Kieran O'Malley, an associate of Brother David who contributed immeasurably to the proceedings by cooking and tending the tape recorder.

A schedule was promptly established. Each day began and ended with half an hour of zazen, seated Zen practice, using meditation cushions Aitken Rōshi brought from Honolulu. They dressed formally for this occasion, and the only photograph taken to commemorate the meeting depicts them so attired, standing in the ribbon of yard separating the cabin from the trees. After changing into casual clothes—jeans and a blue work shirt for Aitken Rōshi, a hooded cassock for Brother David—they joined Kieran in the kitchen for breakfast, then settled into wicker chairs in the main room for the first of two daily working sessions. Talking there was tantamount to talking outside, for the room has screen and glass on three sides. The mellifluous calls of Chinese thrushes and the rumble of nearby Pāpala Falls mingled with their words.

At noon, they paused for a lunch that, like all their meals, was unelaborate but spiced with excellent table talk, which often turned up points of departure for the next working session. Before returning to the conversation, they broke for a stroll to the waterfall and perhaps a brief siesta. Remnant Hawaiian stonework along the path to the falls gave Brother David the feeling that they were treading sacred ground, and he later fashioned a rosary from kukui nuts that he gathered as they walked. Aitken Rōshi picked flowers along the way and put them in vases around the main room before sitting down for the afternoon session. When the day's work was over, they had an early supper, did zazen by the glow of kerosene lamps, and soon retired.

At their first session, Aitken Rōshi suggested they start by deciding whether to focus on similarities or differences between the Christian and Buddhist approaches. "It seems to me," Brother David responded, "that we should focus on neither our similarities nor our differences but rather on the subject matter, which we've agreed will be everyday practice. The differences and similarities in our points of view will throw the subject matter into an interesting relief. Let readers draw their own conclusions about our differences and our similarities." Aitken Rōshi concurred, and they commenced without further ado.

The bulk of their conversations, comprising two of the book's three sections, were indeed devoted to matters of everyday practice. In the early going, however, and sporadically throughout the week, they felt the need to address contextual questions, including questions about the nature of religious experience, the role of language and metaphor in expressing and shaping such experience, cultural biases East and West, the relative significance of the Buddha and Christ, and the impact, for better or worse, of religious institutions. These parts of the conversation I have gathered in the first section of the book, supposing that the reader may find it helpful to examine these fundamentals before proceeding to the nuts and bolts of practice. This is not to say that *The Ground We Share* must be read from front to back. Those who prefer to browse will find that they can dip into it rewardingly just about anywhere.

As I worked with the transcripts of their conversations, I came increasingly to appreciate the unusual qualities Aitken Rōshi and Brother David brought to them. That each has plumbed the depths of his own tradition and has also cultivated a high degree of familiarity with the other's religion makes them outstanding candidates for such a dialogue, but in the final analysis, I think, it is their personal capacities—big hearts, keen minds, strong practice—that made them such superb dialogue partners and enabled them to push their conversations far beyond the spongy abstractions that too often characterize interreligious discussion. It would be hard to find another pair of representatives so willing to reveal their private lives, so respectful and yet so rigorous in challenging one another, so ready (even at this late stage in their careers) to accept challenges and to learn from one another.

It says a good deal about their characters that each man perceives the other as having furnished the leadership in their exchange. From Aitken Rōshi's perspective, Brother David took the lead by both instigating their meeting and setting its direction with a list of questions that he prepared in advance and that provided the structure of their talks. Brother David acknowledges preparing and posing most of the questions, but he also remembers that Aitken Rōshi had certain topics he felt it crucial to cover and that these powerful concerns guided the entire conversation. The truth probably is that *both* led and that, in admiring the other's leadership, they have forgotten their own. In terms of conversational dynamics, I think readers will discover that the lead often changes hands but that Aitken Rōshi tends to drive the discussion in the first section of the book, while Brother David usually steers the course in sections two and three.

The conversations have a timeless quality that may be attributed to the serenity of Waipi'o, but they are also informed by the men's sense of the critical juncture that civilization has reached and their intense concern about world events. Just three days before they entered the valley, the Bush administration launched Operation Desert Storm, and for all its media management and razzle-dazzle technology, Brother David and Aitken Rōshi understood it as a piece of thoroughly inglorious bloodletting that would have devastating consequences for yet another oppressed and innocent Third World populace. Naturally, this subject cropped up in their conversations from time to time, and the news they received on returning home so distressed them that they taped an extra segment by telephone (here melded into the last chapter), expanding on comments about social change that they had made.

Apart from this war-provoked addition, they have felt no need to supplement their conversations or otherwise make substantive changes in the words they so freely spoke in Waipiʻo. Brother David remarked afterward that the entire event had an uncanny completeness: "We just sat down and did it. At the end of the week, we were done. It wasn't that time ran out but that we had genuinely completed our task. There were no loose ends." The last words they taped were words of gratitude for the time they had shared together and for the invigoration of mind and spirit that had resulted.

Aitken Rōshi, Brother David, and I join in expressing gratitude here to others whose contributions made the Waipiʻo trip and this book possible: Burt Arriens and Brother Kieran, whose essential assistance has been described above; Susan Gilbert, who borrowed time from her busy life as a physician and mother to engineer the sojourn in Waipiʻo; Linda Beech, who generously made her cabin available and later patiently supplied background information; Jason Binford, transcriber extraordinaire; Professor David Chappell of the Department of Religion at the University of Hawaii, to whom we are deeply indebted for guidance in preparing the bibliography; Nancy Graeff, who read the manuscript with a sharp eye for errors and unclarity;

Michael Brackney, for a devoted and expert indexing job; and Patricia Kossmann, executive editor of Triumph Books, whose kindness and flexibility we have enjoyed throughout.

—N. F.

❧ PART ONE ❧

Foundations of Practice

Religious Experience

ORIGINAL EXPERIENCE AND
CULTURAL INTERPRETATIONS

AITKEN RŌSHI: We've agreed that our main subject will be everyday practice—putting into real life, realizing in daily life, our deepest convictions and ideals—but where do those ideals and convictions come from?

BROTHER DAVID: Ultimately from our deepest experience. That's where all religion is grounded: in experience.

AR: Aldous Huxley believed that a certain "perennial experience" underlies all the great religious traditions—a kind of deep experience that's common to all peoples but that the various traditions have formulated differently. Do you think that's true?

BD: This is a much-disputed question. Although some people I highly respect hold that the religious traditions can't be traced back to one universal experience, my conviction that they can has grown over the years. Of course, no two experiences are ever exactly the same; even two experiences of myself are never the same. But there is something in great religious experience that is identical for all the traditions. Do you agree?

AR: I think it would be difficult to define such an experience, since people interpret things through our own cultural biases or expectations. We know from psychology, for example, that a person working with a Freudian therapist is going to have sexy dreams, while a person with a Jungian therapist is going to have archetypal dreams.

BD: In other words, you feel that our cultural frames of reference are so pervasive that they will always enter into the most original experience. I think that's true, but when all the different frames of reference are superimposed, as if they were so many photographic negatives, there still will be an image that comes through, showing what these experiences all have in common. I would suggest, for instance, that this original experience, this deepest experience, is always blissful, even though it may be reached under very painful circumstances.

AR: Yes—blissful, restful, peaceful.

BD: Another aspect of this experience is a sense of universal belonging. Freud calls this an "oceanic feeling," but it's much more than a feeling; it's an existential reality. You know yourself united with all. All of morality, to my mind, springs from this sense of belonging.

AR: What you call "belonging" *is* another aspect of deepest experience. William James quotes a woman saying, about her experience, "The truths of the Bible seem made for me." That's the experience of making a religion your own.

BD: At that moment, with that experience, it becomes your own.

AR: Yes, and the word *own* is instructive in this connection. It's sometimes used to mean "acknowledge," as in the statement "Yes, that's what I did. I own it." In other words, I acknowledge that what you've said about me is true, but saying "I own it" is expressing it very intimately.

BD: It suggests also that, when we own it, we are the masters. Before we own it, it owns us.

AR: Exactly. Before we own something, whether it be our personal history or our religion, it's something outside us, voices coming from outside. It isn't real to us yet; we haven't realized it.

In Zen Buddhism, *intimacy* is a very important word. In the early Chinese literature of Zen, more than a thousand years ago, it was used as a synonym for the great experience we're talking about, the breakthrough that's more commonly called realization or enlightenment. When you are intimate, you are one with. When you are not intimate, you are in your head. In Japanese, one of the terms for intimacy is *shinsetsu,* which is usually understood to denote kindness or appropriateness. For example, if you bring your hostess a gift, she may say you're very *shinsetsu.* On the surface, she means you're very kind, but on a deeper level, she's acknowledging the belonging, the intimacy, that your giving expresses.

BD: Maybe this raises another aspect of this original experience that people from very different traditions and with very different frames of reference would agree on: as a kind of byproduct of the experience, one becomes aware of what it means to be human.

AR: Yes—and also what it means to be this particular human.

BD: That's very interesting. It's both, wouldn't you say? This particular human as united with all others. If, in this experience, each of us realizes what it means to be fully human, then either this experience is universal and is one for all of us, or we'd have to allow for radically different possibilities in being human. We'd have to say, in essence, that there isn't a common human-

ity that unites all people, and that would lead to absolutely dias-
trous consequences.

AR: The deepest experience, though, is one of being united with
all other beings, not just with all other people.

BD: Yes, all other beings, but that doesn't invalidate the point
about our common humanity.

AR: Not at all. The reality of our common humanity comes
home to us when we visit what is, superficially, a foreign culture. Observing and taking part in customs that have evolved
separately from our own, we gradually come to recognize how
they work, how they fit the human condition and express our
"common sense." And in the process, we are enlarged.

BD: That's not only true of visiting other cultures but also true
of meeting a different religious tradition.

AR: Religious traditions *are* cultural traditions! That's why different religions formulate the original experience and the path
toward that experience so disparately, giving us life according to
Saint Benedict's Rule on one hand, say, and *kōan* study on the
other.

BD: So the original experience that all of us can have (and that
great religious leaders probably have had in a more profound
way) is joined to the practice by a cultural bridge or, more specifically, by a religious tradition. A friend of mine calls the
bridge "language," arguing that it's language that channels a
tradition and molds future experience. But whatever we choose
to call it, the bridge from the original experience to the practice
shapes the practice in a particular way and, at the same time,
enables us to trace the practice back to its common root in original experience.

COMMON TERRITORY, DIFFERING VISTAS

AR: I'm sure you know the famous dictum "All paths lead to
the top of the same mountain." This was a favorite expression

of Alan Watts and is a capsulization of a thoughtful essay on comparative religion by A. K. Coomaraswamy titled "Paths That Lead to the Same Summit." The phrase oversimplifies Coomaraswamy's ideas, and I think it's mistaken.

BD: I was just going to say so myself. Why exactly would you say that they don't lead to the top of the same mountain? Why is the image inadequate?

AR: The paths may stop halfway. The paths really lead to a certain experience that differs in depth for each individual.

BD: I see. When I heard this first from Baker Rōshi,[1] he commented, "I don't like the idea that all paths meet in one point. I'd rather say that all paths lose themselves in the same territory." I immediately said I didn't like this expression either because it reminds me of the saying "All roads lead to Rome"—not something I like to hear. The territory is so vast that no one path can do justice to it. This way of reframing the image allows us to live very peacefully with the fact that different traditions may say very different things; they are exploring the same territory but in very different areas.

AR: True—and some of the traditions explore a particular area quite fully, while others will only touch upon that area and concentrate their exploration elsewhere.

BD: That's right. It's recognizably the same ground that we're exploring, but it's so vast that large differences may turn up in what we find. What would you call that ground?

AR: How about the realm of practice?

BD: This is an extremely interesting twist that you've given the question. When we started talking about it, I had a clear scheme in mind: on one side the territory of original experience, on the other practice, and between them the religious tradition or cul-

---

[1] American Zen teacher Richard Baker, former abbot of the San Francisco Zen Center.

ture or language, which serves as a bridge. But you've turned this all around. If I understand you correctly, you're saying that we don't use the bridge to cross back to explore the experience but rather that we go forward into practice, and that very practice is the exploration of the experience. That's a very interesting twist.

A R: The experience actually is momentary, the pure experience itself.

B D: Actually, not even momentary. It's timeless.

A R: In terms of time, it's a point—as in the geometrical definition of a point: it has no dimensions. Students come to me reporting a genuine experience, and they say, "But it was over in a flash," and I say, "Yes, that's true."

B D: And now it will take a lifetime to explore.

A R: Exactly! As Dōgen Zenji emphasized, practice is itself enlightenment.[2]

THE TURNABOUT

B D: Several times we've referred to a great experience at the root of everything. It's important that we refer to it as experience, stressing that it's not an abstract doctrine or something of that sort. On the other hand, nowadays there's an inflation of the term *experience*. People tend to imagine that it's always a big-bang experience, that the moment of religious experience must be something that knocks you over. Perhaps we can counter this tendency by speaking of the notion of an awareness instead of experience, of an existential awareness—our deepest awareness.

A R: In Christianity, don't you have the term *metanoia?* Isn't that a turning around? We have exactly the same term in Buddhism:

---

[2] Dōgen Kigen, a renowned thirteenth-century Japanese Zen master of the Sōtō school.

ekō, a turning around. In his "Song of Zazen," Hakuin Zenji refers to this experience as "turning yourself about and confirming your own self-nature—self-nature that is no nature."[3] It's a unique awareness, all right, but I think the fact that it's a shift should be emphasized.

BD: Yes, that's very good. *Metanoia,* often translated as "conversion," could just as well be translated "thinking upside down," meaning a sudden insight that turns everything upside down.

AR: Exactly. The other term in Japanese is *kenshō,* which means "seeing nature." The implication is seeing into the true nature of things, where inner and outer are not different.

BD: Maybe we could say our deepest insight into reality, as it really is.

AR: Yasutani Rōshi used to say that having kenshō is like rubbing a clear place in a piece of frosted glass: it allows you a peek at true nature, but you need to go on to wipe the whole glass clean and maybe even push it out.[4]

BD: Kenshō is just a first little glimpse?

AR: Yes, Yasutani Rōshi used the Japanese word that means *peek* or *glimpse,* and he mimed rubbing a spot on the frosted pane, then putting his eye to the spot, peering out, and saying, "Oh, that's true nature, all right!" The point is that kenshō gives us a genuine glimpse of true nature but just a glimpse, requiring expansion and clarification.

In some religions, an experience of insight into reality is taken as a be-all, end-all experience. To the Zen student, it's a new beginning—not the very beginning but a new beginning.

---

[3] Hakuin Ekaku, illustrious eighteenth-century Japanese Zen master of the Rinzai school. The text mentioned is translated in Robert Aitken, *Encouraging Words: Zen Buddhist Teachings for Western Students* (New York: Pantheon, 1993), pp. 179–80.
[4] Yasutani Hakuun was founder of the Sanbō Kyodan and taught both Aitken Rōshi and Brother David. See the Introduction.

Thereafter, the task is to deepen and clarify that experience, which is a lifetime process.

BD: In your book *The Dragon That Never Sleeps,* you refer to "the one that cannot wobble."[5] Finding the one within that cannot wobble—is that part of the turnabout experience?

AR: It seems to me that with kenshō you do not necessarily find the one that cannot wobble. The one that cannot wobble is one who has cultivated that initial peek over long, long years.

BD: Maybe you can say that with kenshō you find the one that cannot wobble but that you do not embody it.

AR: That's right. It's interesting that in the Ten Oxherding Pictures,[6] kenshō is picture number three: glimpsing the ox. Lassoing the ox, taming the ox, riding the ox, turning the ox loose, and so on are all subsequent steps in the process.

BD: And this process is practice. Our deepest existential insights are translated by practice into everyday living.

AR: Absolutely. Even *anuttara-samyak-sambodhi*—supreme, all-encompassing enlightenment—is practice.

BD: When you say that, do you mean that unless you translate it into your own life's reality, it's just an idea or a memory, something lifeless?

AR: Exactly. Do you know the kōan about stepping from the top of a hundred-foot pole? Unfortunately, a number of books turn the kōan around so that it seems quite meaningless, but in reality the person on top of the pole is a person who's stuck on enlightenment, stuck in an experience of emptiness, and the question is, how do you step from the top of that hundred-foot pole?

---

[5] *The Dragon That Never Sleeps* (Berkeley: Parallax Press, 1992) is a book of verses for practice.

[6] A ten-frame representation of the stages of Zen practice that is most often credited to the twelfth-century Chinese master K'uo-an Chih-yuan.

BD: That's good. The parallel Christian episode comes after the Transfiguration, when the disciples have to leave the mountain, Mount Tabor. The Transfiguration is the kenshō, and the disciples immediately want to stay there. They say, "Oh, this is like the Feast of the Tabernacle! Let's build three tabernacles here and celebrate. Let's stay here." But then it's all over, and as they descend the mountain, Jesus says to them, "Don't tell anybody of this vision until the Son of Man is risen from the dead." [Mt. 7:1–13] First you have to go through the suffering, then you can talk about the experience.

In the sixties, when mystical literature started booming in the West, *Ascent of Mount Carmel* by St. John of the Cross was the book that everyone had to read. My first abbot and the founder of our order, Father Damasus Winzen, used to say, "The great task isn't the ascent of Mount Carmel. The great task is the descent from Mount Tabor." The ascent of Mount Carmel leads to the hundred-foot pole, and you must then get down from that. A wonderful saying from the early monks also applies here: "When you see a monk going up to heaven, pull him down by his legs!"

ℵ 2 ⅃

Self and the Ultimate

The Mystery of the Self

BROTHER DAVID: In our culture, we speak of being self-centered as a character flaw, but where else should we be centered, if not in the self? Everything depends, of course, on which self you mean. Normally, the word *self-centered* refers to the little self, which cares only for itself and does not deserve to be the center. But we can also find a positive interpretation of self-centeredness—namely, coming from the heart, not being ex-centric, not losing yourself outside somewhere but really being rooted within your innermost center.

AITKEN RŌSHI: I think so. Each of us has a responsibility to take care of ourselves—to care for the self as a Buddha, not even as an avatar of the Buddha but actually as a Buddha.

BD: As the Buddha.

AR: As *the* Buddha, in all modesty. It's up to me to take care of this Buddha—to avoid catching cold, to keep myself adequately fed and clothed, to get a good night's sleep, to have the right kind of work, and so on. Is that self-centered? I think that's the light side of self-centeredness.

But we need to say something here about the nature of the self. The popular idea is that in Buddhism there *is* no self. A more complete expression would be that there is no self, and the *self* realizes this fact. To put it another way, no-self and self are complementary. A similar point can be made about existence: people understand superficially that, according to Buddhism, nothing exists. In actuality, nothing exists, and that is the nature of what we see.

Existence and nonexistence, self and no-self—these are complementarities, like the notion of light as waves and the notion of light as particles. Both notions are correct at the same time. But if we get stuck on light as particles, then we can't see it as waves. If we get stuck on matter as eternally substantial, then we can't see it as empty. It's important that we see into the emptiness in order to fully appreciate the substance.

BD: There would be a parallel, although it may not be so obvious in the way in which I will try to express it, in the Christian understanding of reality. It starts with Jesus preaching and with the people's first understanding of him as a prophet: here is someone who tells about God, the altogether Other—the nothing, you might say, over against everything. The next step of the understanding was that this man Jesus so totally conveys this divine reality that we will not call him a messenger. We will call him "the Word." He is simply Word. Everything he does, everything he says, is Word, is full expression of the altogether Other. The next step is, in the words of the prologue of John's Gospel, that in the beginning—before "always"—was the Word, and that Word was with God and, finally, *was* God. This is like being and nonbeing: being expresses nonbeing, is with nonbeing, and finally *is* nonbeing.

AR: Can we acknowledge that this tends to be complicated and that it might lead to the idea that ultimately there really is such a thing as God separate from us, from beings?

BD: Yes, not only we acknowledge it, but history bears out that the great trap of the Western religious traditions—Judaism,

Islam, and Christianity—is dualism. That is our great trap. There may be a parallel trap, the opposite trap, in the Eastern traditions, which would be monism, the idea of oneness. I'm more sensitive to our own trap in the West, but the reason I would call monism a trap is that it, too, fails to do justice to experience. In particular, it doesn't allow space for gratefulness.

AR: I think that monism is far too limited a term for the Eastern view. The vast emptiness referred to in Buddhism, actually experienced in practice, isn't a vacuum. It's full of possibilities, charged with potential, always springing forth in a myriad of varied, particular forms. This gives the lie to the New Age aphorism that it's all one, all God.

Moreover, the fact that mountains and rivers and trees and people and cities spring forth as they do can only evoke gratitude in anyone who is really open to the world. In Japan, the expression *arigatai* is pervasive. This is the root of the word *arigatō*—"thank you." Japanese people respond to a spectacular sunrise by saying, *Arigatai na,* which roughly translates, "It's very gratifying, isn't it!"

BD: I knew this, and I'm happy you expressed it so well. I certainly don't want to paint the Eastern tradition as actually monistic. I just said that it's a trap, a danger. Similarly, dualism is only a trap for Western tradition; the Western tradition is not dualistic fundamentally or inherently. It is heresy, total distortion, to call it dualistic. Even by its own testimony, the Christian tradition is trinitarian.

I wish that the Trinity, which is so central to Christian tradition, would be taken more as a focus of experiential teaching! Unfortunately, when it's mentioned at all, it's usually presented as beyond our grasp: "Well, this is a great mystery. Don't bother about it. You'll never understand it anyway." In reality, yes, it *is* the most profound mystery, but it's exactly what we're aware of in our deepest experiences. It's not three somethings sitting out there somewhere: It's me over here, being very specific—very real in this sense, very different and unique—experiencing being the altogether Other. Not simply being the altogether Other but being one with the altogether Other. It's this something, me, being one with nothing and experiencing, at the same time, that my aliveness—to use that term for the lack of a better one—is the aliveness of this Other that is not other.

I'm groping for words here, but that's the dynamics of it. The *experience* is clearly trinitarian. The trinitarian dogmas weren't formulated in order to describe some divine object out there. They were formulated to describe the divine structure of every human being's innermost experience.

The Multicentered Self and the Cosmic Christ

AR: In opening our discussion of self-centeredness, you spoke of the small self, implying opposition to a large self. I think of the large self as the multicentered self. I myself am that multicentered self, as you are, as everyone is, as everything is, every leaf on every tree. Every cell contains all cells, so when I take care of myself, with true awareness of the Buddha, I am taking care of all selves.

BD: That's one of those deep insights into the truth that probably is expressed in many traditions. In the Christian tradition, it finds its expression when Saint Paul says of himself, as a person who has achieved the turnabout experience, that conversion we spoke of, "I live, yet not I. Christ lives in me." [Gal. 2:20] Of course, he means the cosmic Christ, the Christ that lives in Paul and lives in Peter and lives in you and lives in the animals and the plants. Having found that cosmic Christ as living within you, as the life of your life, means having found that center that has its center everywhere.

AR: It's too bad Paul didn't explicate it the way you have!

BD: Well, it's pretty obvious. It's not that Paul didn't make it clear enough. I think the tradition just hasn't picked up that particular passage sufficiently.

AR: It looks as though "Jesus Christ lives in me"—the spirit of the man, so to speak.

BD: Well, the relationship between the historic Christ and what I call the cosmic Christ is very subtle. You could say that the historic Jesus was totally alive with the cosmic Christ reality but did not exhaust that reality. Each one of us, when we find our fulfillment, is totally filled with the Christ reality, but none of us exhausts the Christ reality because that is the spirit or the life of the totality.

AR: I confess to some discomfort with the term *Christ reality*. I wonder if it can explode, if it will self-destruct, the way that equivalent expressions in Buddhism self-destruct. Can you express Christ reality, "not I but Christ lives in me," without using the name of a person?

BD: "Christ" *isn't* the name of a person. It's a title like "Buddha." So to say "Christ reality" is a perfect parallel to saying "Buddha nature."

AR: Okay, but is it possible to answer as Chao-chou did, for example, when he was asked about the Buddha nature of a dog?[1] He answered in the negative: "Has the dog Buddha nature or not?" Chao-chou said, "No"—*mu,* in Japanese. In other words, there's no such thing as Buddha nature.

BD: That's really what he's saying, not that the dog doesn't have it.

AR: Yes. But the *mu,* the "no" itself, has a certain reality, has a certain power. That power lives on, and so the question a student works with in studying this kōan is, "What is *mu?*"

---

[1] Chao-chou Ts'ung-shen, eminent Zen master of ninth-century China. The dialogue quoted is the first case of *The Gateless Barrier,* a classical Zen text.

BD: I see. I have one other question before I can fully answer. I want to be fairly safe and ask you first, in what way do similar Buddhist terms self-destruct?

AR: Since we're talking about the nature of the self, take the example of the three bodies of the Buddha: the Dharmakāya, the pure, clear, empty body of the Buddha; the Sambhogakāya, the blissful, harmonious body; and the Nirmānakāya, the varied and unique body. These three bodies are not separate; we speak of them as separate aspects just for purposes of explication. This unique, particular body is at the same time the harmonious body of all and empty, which is to say, in experiential terms, at peace.

The Sambhogakāya cannot stand alone as a metaphor. It can only be taken in the framework of Buddhist metaphysics. It is not an independent reality. As soon as you speak of the Sambhogakāya, the Nirmānakāya appears. And the Nirmānakāya is totally opposite to the Sambhogakāya. The Nirmānakāya is the unique, independent nature of everything and everybody, completely alone in the whole universe, when everything else disappears. Like all religious experience, this is momentary. Even the terms for it do not abide.

BD: We even have an interesting parallel, too esoteric for us to work out here, between the Three Bodies of the Buddha and the Holy Trinity. Not just because it's three—there's a lot more to it.

Anyway, what you said enables me to answer your question. The key word, which you've introduced, is metaphysics. We've already agreed that the experience from which the Buddhist and Christian traditions both come is the one, ultimate human experience, not two different experiences. But the metaphysics of these two traditions, the way they speak about the experience and understand it even, are diametrically opposed.

AR: I'll agree to that.

BD: So, answering your question in the context of Christian metaphysics, I have to say that the cosmic Christ, the reality of the cosmic Christ, cannot be exploded. It doesn't self-destruct. That stands to reason. In Buddhist metaphysics, any parallel concept would have to self-destruct because Buddhism is centered around negation, the emptiness and the silence, above all the silence. It is a tradition of silence as, for example, when the Buddha holds up a flower and says no words, in the so-called Flower Sermon.

AR: That's very expressive, however!

BD: Yes, it's an expressive silence.

AR: It's an expressive *presentation,* not an expressive silence.

BD: So silence is not very important there?

AR: No, not at all. The presentation just happens to be silent.

BD: Doesn't it appear to you, as it appears to me, that in the Christian tradition the word is everything—the yes, the word, the positive—and that the Buddhist tradition reciprocally stresses the other side—the negation, the silence? I see these two as inseparably connected; the one could not be without the other. The human mind is too limited to have everything in one tradition, so there has to be another tradition than Christianity that carries, equally, the silence.

AR: I think that's too simple. In Buddhism, emptiness is stressed because emptiness is the less evident partner in the complementarity of emptiness and form. A Zen Buddhist is conscious all the time that he or she is a living embodiment of that tension, that creativity, that complementarity, which is an intellectual paradox but not any other kind of paradox. There *is* no paradox in nature. A Buddhist cannot take metaphysics seriously because he or she knows that the truth of metaphysics is only as true as the truth of no metaphysics, while Christians, I think, tend to take metaphysics seriously. In other words, a Christian can never say there's no such thing as Christ.

BD: I understand what you're driving at now, and I'm very grateful for this exchange. I think now I can answer your question much more simply and directly. Let's go once more back to your question: in Christianity, can the concept of "Christ" self-destruct? I'm convinced, since both traditions come from the same experiential awareness, that it must be possible for me to find this point expressed somewhere in Christianity. In other words, although obviously there is far less emphasis of this point in Christianity than in Buddhism, I must be able to demonstrate to you that, yes, the concept of "Christ" can self-destruct in some way or another.

I found the way to do this while we were talking. In the fifteenth chapter of First Corinthians [1 Cor. 15:26], Saint Paul says that in the end, by which he means the ultimate realm, "when everything has been subjected to Christ," which can only refer to the cosmic Christ, not the historical Jesus, "then also death will be subjected to Christ." Life, death, everything is subjected, then—and this is the salient point—the cosmic Christ will hand over the kingdom to the Father, and God, who is the silence out of which the Word came in the beginning, will be all in all. At that point, the Word returns to the Silence.

AR: Pardon me if I have a niggling doubt. Can you acknowledge that God is a concept?

BD: God is a name for a reality that cannot be named.

AR: Okay!

BD: But the decisive thing in this context is that God is the Silence from which the Word comes in the beginning, and to which the Word returns in the end. That's the background to this. The Word enters back into the Silence, and then God will be all in all.

AR: And in that ultimate, God *is* all in all. It's not a matter of time or sequence.

BD: No, of course, it's really not, and that expresses so beautifully what you call "self-destructing." It's not the kind of self-destructing that occurs when somebody blows himself up. It's a self-destructing that is, really, ultimate fulfillment.

AR: Yes. *The Diamond Sutra* and all other teachings in Buddhism that destroy or wipe away concepts are intended to show how limited those concepts are. It's not that these concepts in some way return to the source but rather that, in the context of the source, which is all-encompassing, all concepts are limited.

BD: In other words, you're not even talking about the reality behind the concepts but only about the self-destruction of the concepts. I thought you were talking about more.

AR: But the reality behind the concepts is also in front of the concepts, on all sides, and in between.

BD: You're saying a lot more than that concepts are inadequate to express the reality for which they stand. You're saying nonbeing and being are exchangeable.

AR: Yes, exactly. Nonbeing and being are exchangeable.

BD: That's what I had in mind. As Thomas Aquinas says, "The act with which God," the Silence, "speaks the eternal Word is the same act with which God creates the world." God is too simple to have more than one act. The speaking of the Word is the "yes" and the positive of everything; everything is created in and through the Word. When the Word—the Son—hands back everything there is to the Father, then the Word returns into the Silence, and God will be all in all. This myth-image created by Saint Paul is one way of looking, in Christian terms, at the relationship of being and nonbeing. Admittedly, it hasn't been highly developed in the Christian tradition, but all we need is to find a foothold.

AR: Exactly, you need a foothold and then to express it a little more simply. In time, as Christianity evolves through contact with other world religions, surely that rather complicated expression will be simplified. I find it quite difficult to grasp.

BD: It is, of course, mythic language. Saying that everything is subject to the Son and that he will hand over the kingdom to the Father—it's deeply mythic. But is it so difficult to grasp what stands behind it?

AR: No, I don't think so. Of course, our responsibility in this dialogue is to find our points of difference as well as our points of agreement. This may be one of them. In *The Blue Cliff Record,* a monk asks Chao-chou, "All things return to the One. Where does the One return?"[2] The word *return* is a literal translation of the Chinese, but both the Chinese word and its Japanese equivalent may also mean "come down to" or "amount to" as well as "return to" or "come back to." So the question might be translated, "All things amount to the One. What does the One amount to?" Chao-chou gives a very metaphorical answer, which we needn't go into. The monk's question is the one we're up against here, isn't it? There is no "returning to" in the sense of a "handing back" from Word to Silence. "All things are really One. So then what is the One?" Can you answer?

BD: I know a kōan is to be answered from a different level, but speculatively, I'd say that the One amounts to all things.

AR: That's the correct interpretive response. Of course, there's a kōan response as well, but you're correct. That's the way it goes: All things come down to One. What does the One come down to? It comes down to all things.

In contrast to this kind of pithy statement, I find your expression—or Saint Paul's expression—awfully complex. It sounds as though there were some kind of transaction involving time and involving space.

BD: Now I understand what you meant by doing it a little more simply. I felt as if I had, with ultimate effort, climbed up to the

---

[2] *The Blue Cliff Record:* a classical Zen text. The dialogue quoted is from Case 45. For a translation, see Thomas and J. C. Cleary (Boston: Shambhala, 1992).

roof and done a handstand up there, and you said, "Quite nice, but can't you do it a little more simply?"

It's very difficult. This isn't something that's very obvious in the Christian tradition. I have no problem identifying differences between the two traditions, but I'd have an enormous problem accepting differences that were opposed instead of complementary. It just doesn't fit my worldview. I've never come across such a thing, and I don't expect ever to come across it.

If I were to discover an apparent opposition between the two traditions, it would merely make me say, "Well, I haven't fully understood it. I know that when I understand it, I'll see it as complementary." I come to our discussion with this preconceived frame of reference. If you can accept it, fine. If you can't. . . .

AR: I accept it, and in the *practice,* which we agree is most important, there's plenty of evidence for the apophatic, the tradition of the Silence, in the Christian tradition. When Brother Peter, novice master at Our Lady of Guadalupe, described his meditation to me, it sounded exactly the same as *shikantaza.*[3] In fact, it *is* exactly the same.

BD: And that's not an individual case. For centuries, the Church has had what we call Prayer of Silence or Prayer of Union. It's widely practiced, especially these days. Existentially and experientially, as you rightly say, it's the apophatic, experiential aspect of Christianity.

WHAT DISAPPEARS, WHAT REMAINS

BD: In one of his books, William Johnston writes about going to *dokusan* at a *sesshin* that he attended.[4] When the teacher asked

---

[3] Our Lady of Guadalupe: a Trappist monastery in Lafayette, Oregon, where Aitken Rōshi conducted sesshin in the 1970s. Shikantaza (lit., "nothing other than just sitting"): a form of Zen practice that is particularly associated with the Sōtō tradition.

[4] Contemporary Jesuit priest and author of several books on Buddhism and Christianity. See the appendix for titles of relevant works. Dokusan: a one-to-one interview with a Zen teacher, also called *sanzen.* Sesshin: a Zen retreat.

how he was doing, Johnston answered, "To put it in Christian terms, I'm just sitting there in the presence of God." That's it—silent prayer in the presence of God.

The teacher said, "That's good. Just keep sitting, and before you know it, God will disappear and only Johnston-san will be sitting there."

Father Johnston said, "To me it seems that Johnston would disappear, and only God would remain."

"That's right!" the teacher answered. "Exactly what I said."

It's a good story, illustrating the common experience at the heart of the two traditions and also what "remains" in this experience—nothing out there, just our quest. Our engagement on this path remains, even though we don't know who we are, don't know where we're going, don't know where we're coming from. When Saint Paul says, "I live, yet not I. Christ lives in me," he's giving the name "Christ" to that reality that's still sitting there on the mat when everything else disappears.

AR: I'd express it like this: continue your sitting, and you'll find that only the song of the thrush and the cry of the gecko are sitting there. Only the scent of the incense is sitting there.

BD: I have no difficulty understanding that. My difficulty, my groping with all this, stems from your question, "How does that experience relate to the Christian tradition?" Your question was whether I can let go of the cosmic Christ.

AR: That's right.

BD: Let's approach the question from another angle. A long time ago, I was sought out by a Christian sister of a religious order who was doing intensive Zen practice. She'd been told by a teacher to let go of everything and found herself in a dilemma: how could she possibly let go of Christ? I got in some trouble for telling her that there was absolutely no question that she was obliged to let go of Christ and that she didn't have to worry the least bit because anything important about Christ would only come to her after she let go.

I lost track of her thereafter, so I don't know whether she did it, but that's my conviction: We have to let go of anything that we can understand as Christ out there, have to let go of anything we can possibly hang onto. Only then will that come forth which we don't need to hang on to, that which is there without our hanging on to it. This is what I understand Saint Paul to refer to when he says, "I live, yet not I. Christ lives in me." *That* will be realized only after a person has let go of everything that we can possibly let go.

In this sense, when you ask, "Can a Christian let go of the cosmic Christ?" my answer would be, "Yes, we can let go of any concept, including that of the cosmic Christ. We must let go of every concept." But this notion of the cosmic Christ refers to that which remains after letting everything go. Or you can say it refers to that which does the letting go. You can let go of the notion, but the reality indicated by the term *cosmic Christ* is that which lets go and that which one can't lose.

AR: But when there's only the song of the thrush, everything, even awareness of the song, has disappeared.

BD: Sure, it's disappeared. That has to do with knowing. When you do let go, you don't know anything remains.

AR: So the knowing really is after the fact.

BD: Right. In fact it has disappeared. That would be one way of understanding: that everything has disappeared.

I'm not doing a particularly good job of linking this with Christian tradition, I'm afraid. The Christian tradition has a completely different perspective and metaphysics, so it's very difficult to express it in these terms. But at least to my own satisfaction, I find enough foothold in what has been explicitly said within the Christian tradition to know that we aren't dealing with two incompatible realities or notions but rather are experiencing—and talking in two complementary ways about— one and the same reality. Do you believe that?

AR: Yes, I think it's true. The expressions, the metaphysics, of the two traditions have very different configurations, so it's probably not possible to find large patterns of similarity, but I do see similarities when comparisons are drawn point by point, with great care and at a high level of detail.

BD: Since this hasn't really been worked out in the Christian tradition, we're at a historic beginning here. I don't necessarily mean right here, in this little cottage in Waipi'o Valley, although that may also be true; I mean that our conversations are part of a larger process that's still in its early stages.

I'm very happy that the intersection between our traditions really is there to be found. We aren't betraying ourselves as Christians if we find it. It can be found with some goodwill and developed from here on. You're right on that point, too, I think: it must be developed and will be developed, undoubtedly, in the future. Under the influence of Buddhist metaphysics and so forth, Christians will have to do a lot of reflection.

Knowledge, Wisdom, and Heart

THE USES AND LIMITATIONS OF KNOWLEDGE

BROTHER DAVID: As we've already agreed, deep religious experience requires a letting go, a surrender to not knowing. To take that a little further, it might be useful to distinguish between knowledge and wisdom. Many sincere religious seekers have been sidetracked by knowledge about religious life, religious doctrine, and so on. We need to say to them, in all sympathy, "Okay, you like to learn, but what you're after is wisdom. No amount of knowledge will get you to wisdom."

AITKEN RŌSHI: In this connection, I think of Simone Weil and particularly of an essay in her book *Waiting for God* that's titled "Reflections on the Right Use of School Studies with a View to the Love of God."[1] At one point in her multifaceted career, she had been a schoolteacher, and in the essay, she describes how she trained students to give attention to their studies. She says, for instance, that when she asked students to pay

---

[1] Noted twentieth-century, lay Catholic thinker, activist, and social critic.

attention, they looked very serious but weren't really paying attention; they were just tensing their muscles. Knowing very well what quality of attention was necessary for the religious path, she encouraged her students to cultivate that quality of attention to their studies, hoping this might lead some of them to deeper things later on. Ultimately, she seems to be saying, the quality of attention that a true scholar has can be a valuable foundation for religious practice. In that sense, the pursuit of knowledge can lead, just as a simple next step, to the pursuit of wisdom.

BD: But at best it's a preparatory step. Knowledge or the quality of your attention doesn't directly lead you to wisdom.

AR: True. Yet I don't want to undervalue knowledge. Knowledge may continually inform us as we walk the path of wisdom.

BD: That is very important. I just want to emphasize that knowledge and the acquisition of knowledge are always only preparatory and do not lead you as a next step in a straight line to wisdom. For wisdom, you have to turn around completely, abandoning so-called knowledge. What flashes through my mind is a passage from Saint Bernard of Clairvaux's commentary on the Song of Songs.[2] I don't remember the exact wording, but the translation would be something like this: What you can grasp gives you knowledge. What grasps *you* makes you wise.

AR: Exactly! Here we return to the song of the thrush and the cry of the gecko: they grasp us, and we disappear. Dōgen Zenji said, "That the self advances and confirms the ten thousand things is called delusion. That the ten thousand things advance and confirm the self is enlightenment." It's exactly the same point that Saint Bernard made.

BD: This being-grasped-by is also the essence of our most typically Benedictine method of formal practice, which is Lectio Divina, or spiritual reading. This kind of reading is not geared

---

[2] A leading French monk and reformer of the eleventh century, later canonized.

toward acquisition of knowledge but rather toward allowing the text to take hold of you. You are encouraged not to read as much as you can as quickly as you can but, on the contrary, to read very slowly and definitely no more than you absolutely need. If the first word turns you on, that's better than if you have to read a whole sentence. You just lay yourself open and allow the text to take hold of you and to carry you where it will.

Another thing that came to mind from my own experience and preference relates to what you said about nourishing your wisdom with learning. The kind of reading that most nourishes my particular spirituality is poetry (not necessarily religious poetry) and nature study—books about astronomy, botany, and zoology, books like *The Lives of a Cell* by Lewis Thomas. I'm sure what nourishes us varies greatly from one person to another, but to my mind, poetry and nature writing make wonderful spiritual nourishment.

AR: I agree. I also love wise commentaries on classical texts, essays by people who have digested those old texts. For example, Tu Wei-ming has opened my eyes rather late to the profound possibilities of Confucianism. A book I've been reading lately, *The Water of Life,* does this with Hawaiian mythology. The author, a Jungian psychologist named Rita Knipe, has digested Hawaiian myths through maybe a decade of study, then retold them in her own words from a Jungian perspective.

BD: That's a good caution, I think: one doesn't have to go directly to the original sacred texts. Beginners, in their enthusiasm, often go to the primary texts and then are really disappointed or, equally dangerous, misunderstand and misinterpret them. I always feel a little uneasy when people discovering or rediscovering the Christian faith tell me, "I'm so enthusiastic now, I'm reading the Bible from beginning to end!" Of course, sooner or later that's very helpful and healthy, but for people young in their faith and practice, opening the Bible just anywhere and beginning to read, without a commentary, may be very problematic.

AR: Let me comment about the dark side of knowledge. Some scholars—not all, but some—tend to slot their knowledge, to fit facts into a worldview that they are gradually evolving from their reading. The upshot can be a structure so tightly interconnected that no real inspiration can come through. I think this is a great danger. It's for this reason that the old teachers in my tradition sometimes said, "Don't read." Even some American teachers of Zen, I know, have discouraged reading.

BD: In the Christian tradition, too, in recent centuries some fervent contemplative communities were very anti-intellectual. Now that has changed, but I think it was for similar reasons, and this raises another aspect of this question about knowledge and wisdom: knowledge *may* lead one in the direction of wisdom as a preparatory development, and it *may* later inform and nourish wisdom, but is it necessary? Does one have to be something of an intellectual in order to become wise? What about the wisdom of the elders in, for all intents and purposes, illiterate cultures?

AR: The peasant who is wise in the way of the soil and the seasons has a cosmic wisdom, there's no question about it. In our own country, I think of the Amish and the wisdom that writers and thinkers like Wendell Berry find in their very down-to-earth ways. My intention in citing Simone Weil was really to make the point that scholarly learning isn't necessarily at odds with the path of wisdom.

BD: Of course. I just want to emphasize, for the benefit of readers who are likely to pick up the kind of book that we're working on here—readers who will tend to be intellectual or to pay attention to learning—that knowledge isn't necesarily a door to wisdom and that it can also be a block. The decisive thing about finding wisdom—I don't want to say "acquiring" wisdom because one doesn't acquire it; one finds it—is opening yourself to receive, to be grasped, to be touched by the thrush and gecko.

A R : To be *occupied* by the thrush and gecko.

B D : To be occupied. To be preoccupied. It doesn't come through our reaching out and grasping. In Christian terminology, such an experience of being grasped or occupied would be placed under the heading of the supernatural. This has nothing to do with the occult. Basically, the divine realm is called the supernatural; everything else is just the natural. To avoid conceptions of a sort of two-storied universe—with the divine above and ordinary below—and yet to maintain this traditional distinction, which speaks about something quite valid, I consider the natural as everything that we can grasp and the supernatural as that which grasps us.

In our daily experience, mostly we come across things that we can grasp in some way or other. Of course, there are always things we can't grasp intellectually because we haven't learned to do so. That's a different story. Because my mechanical mind is so little developed, I don't even grasp how a toilet works; this is beyond my grasp right now, but sooner or later, I know, at least theoretically I'd be able to grasp that. That belongs in the realm of the natural. The supernatural is that which, by definition, we cannot grasp and which takes hold of us. I believe that this reality, the supernatural, is in every person's experience.

A R : I think use of the term *super* does imply, to the uninitiated, a two-storied universe. But certainly I think we could say, accepting your terminology, that the experience of the thrush occupying me is supernatural.

B D : I would say that "the thrush occupying me" is your description of coming in touch with the supernatural. That's all we can ever hope to do—say how we came in touch with it.

A R : In the words of one of my students, "When I turned over in bed, there was nothing at all."

BD: That was an encounter with the supernatural.

AR: In Buddhism, we would say it's just the natural.

BD: Well, you interpret supernatural as above the natural, but that's not the only way the word can be understood. *Super* may mean "above us," but it may also be simply an intensifier. We can say, for example, that one thing is fine and another is super-fine, meaning even finer than the first. In the same sense, one experience may be natural while another is supernatural. *Natural* derives from the verb "nasci," to be born. In the sense I intend, the supernatural is closer to birth—to the source from which everything gushes forth—than the merely natural.

HAVING HEART

BD: I think there's a parallel between the *supernatural,* in this sense, and the word *intimacy,* which you spoke of as a synonym in Chinese Zen for *enlightenment* or *realization.* It's the opposite of separation or alienation. In this connection, I want to pose a question that one of your students suggested we consider in our conversations, a question about heart. He said, "In the years of my Zen practice, I've known a lot of meditators, and I've seen that rigorous practice does not necessarily lead to a presence in the heart. Power, *hara,*[3] or whatever can often predominate. Some meditators have no presence at all of that kind." Is presence in the heart a goal of Zen practice? Where does it fit?

AR: In this sense of *heart,* presence in the heart is certainly a goal of Zen practice, but in many Zen centers hara is empha-sized more. Hara is the power engendered by deep concentra-tion, by settling oneself in one's belly, and like power of other kinds, it may be used for better or for worse. Projecting this

---

[3] Japanese term (literally, "belly" or "guts") commonly used to denote one's per-sonal center and source of strength. Used in Zen especially to indicate the lower abdomen as the physical center of practice.

power through competition in the world, innocuously through martial arts or perniciously through manipulation of others, is a feature found in certain Zen centers, no question about it. I'm very doubtful about such things, and from the beginning, my emphasis has been on reception and listening, allowing the other to possess me, letting there be only the song of the thrush sitting on my cushions. I put the stress on intimacy rather than on power, if you will.

BD: I'd like you to enlarge on the notion of heart. In the Christian tradition, at the deepest level, we speak of the heart as an equivalent for what we here have called home or the ground we share, the essential ground, the territory of true religious experience.

AR: Roger Corless calls it "the space under the tree."[4]

BD: Yes, that space. That would be heart. It ties in with what you said just now because the heart is the organ of ultimate listening. With our ears we only hear the sound waves of the thrush. To hear the thrush in the sense in which you hear it on your practice cushion, that's listening with the heart.

AR: It's providing a perch for the thrush.

BD: Okay, the heart is a perch for the thrush. And there's a deep significance in calling it the heart: when we speak of our heart, in biblical terms, we mean the whole person—intellect, will, emotion, body, mind. It doesn't mean only our emotions. In the sense it's intended, *heart* stands for the whole person. It has strong emotional overtones because it *is* the whole person, and usually when we speak of a person, particularly in our culture, we leave out all the emotional aspects.

Anyway, in Christian terms our common ground is the Sacred Heart. The heart of the world, the heart of the universe—

---

[4] Contemporary British scholar active in the Buddhist-Christian dialogue and author of *Vision of Buddhism: The Space under the Tree.*

it's what you find when you go to the depths of your own heart. It's the heart of hearts. When we really reach that heart of hearts, we've reached the spot where all hearts are one, the space we call the sacred heart, where your heartbeat is the heartbeat of the universe.

Speaking of it as the heart makes a difference for practice because it warms everything up. Frequently, Christians go to a Zen center and are very happy there, finding everything in their practice that they've always been looking for, yet they miss that personal warmth.

AR: I think that's true—in some Zen centers more than others.

BD: Do you think it's a legitimate need—the need for a warmth and a personal aspect within the practice?

AR: I certainly do. Zen practice tends to be austere by its nature. With its silent sitting, its weeklong sesshin without talking, and so on, we must be very careful to build in ways that encourage intimacy. For example, we always hold hands at the end of a business meeting. We're careful to *gasshō* when greeting one another.[5] We have an informal time of tea and free conversation after every community gathering for zazen.

BD: This also ties in with our preceding conversation about the cosmic Christ. I think part of the reason I had such difficulties with your question "Can the cosmic Christ self-destruct? Can you drop that notion?" is that I heard underneath (and maybe I projected it) the question "Can you drop a personal relationship with the cosmic Christ?" I have no difficulty dropping the term, any term, and in the way we laboriously worked out, I agree that the concept or reality does self-destruct. There's no problem with that.

But in another sense, the idea of the cosmic Christ—the idea

---

[5] Literally, palms placed together. The Zen term for this traditional Asian gesture of greeting, reverence, and gratitude.

that one can have a personal relationship to the ultimate—is so important! Can we drop even that? In the context of the heart, my answer now is, yes, we can also drop the notion of a personal relationship because that's all still in your head, a reflection, something after-the-fact that may be said or felt about the experience.

Still, it seems to me that Christian terms and images such as the Sacred Heart make something explicit about the experience that in other traditions—and Zen may be one of them—isn't made explicit, namely that when you relate to the ultimate in a personal way, it's experienced as mutual. This far transcends any reflexive notions or concept or terminology. It's simply a matter of experience. That's the decisive point: it's both metaphysical (although that's not the aspect that I want to stress) and deeply related to practice. I have a feeling this underlies the question our friend has raised about presence in the heart.

Let me take this a little further. This sense of a personal relatedness with the Ultimate is expressed in Christian terminology by calling the Silence, the altogether Other, father or mother or friend or spouse or lover. We express this relationship with the Ultimate in human terms. I don't know whether it fits at all from your perspective, but to use the metaphor of the Three Bodies of the Buddha, when the varied and unique body calls the clear, empty body friend or father or lover, then the blissful, harmonious body, which we would call the Holy Spirit, makes the whole thing alive.

AR: From the Buddhist point of view the Sambhogakāya, the harmonious body, is the link between the pure, clear Dharmakāya and the varied, unique Nirmānakāya. So there actually is a correspondence here.

BD: It must be so if both Zen and Christianity, like all other religious traditions, are ways to move from our basic human condition to our most unfolded human condition. It's impossible that something that is so profound and so central to one tradition couldn't be there in the other tradition. It must be there somehow, though expressed differently—and that difference is very good, very desirable.

AR: To recap and to express this as simply as possible, what we've acknowledged here is that in Christianity there's a much warmer, personal feeling of relationshp to the Ultimate than in Buddhism. We can see the ramifications of that in Christianity's emphasis on brotherhood and sisterhood and service and mission. The other side of the coin is the more metaphysical side—the cool side, if you will—which has been strongly developed in Buddhism and not so strongly in Christianity.

There's a very interesting story in *The Blue Cliff Record* that touches on the matter of warmth: Ch'ang-sha, an early Chinese Zen master, went for a stroll in the hills.[6] When he came back, the head monk met him at the gate and said, "Where have you been strolling?"

Ch'ang-sha answered, "I've been strolling about in the hills."

"Where did you go?" the monk asked. Actually, the Chinese idiom is, "Where did you come and go?" which has deep layers of implication in Buddhism. Really, it's the coming and going of the whole world.

Ch'ang-sha said, "First I went through the scented grasses. Then I came back following the falling flowers."

The head monk replied, "That's the spring mood itself."

There's a bit of a challenge in the head monk's reply, and Ch'ang-sha ended the exchange with the telling comment, "It's better than autumn dew falling on the lotus blossoms." Here you can see the poetical implication that in Zen Buddhism there's a preference for spring, with its warmth and flowers and fragrance, with the harmony of nature and of human beings in nature.

---

[6] *The Blue Cliff Record,* case 36.

BD: In other words, the whole realm of the heart. It *is* there. Would you admit that it isn't, at least in current practices, sufficiently stressed or developed?

AR: Yes, I would.

BD: I think we should look at the other side, the Christian weakness in the "cool" aspect. It has to be acknowledged in the context of our dialogue here that, though we Christians speak of "theology," which literally means words or teachings about God, what we actually have is almost exclusively teaching about God as known in Jesus Christ and through Jesus Christ and from the point of view of Jesus Christ. In the creed, God is mentioned in the first half-sentence, then not mentioned anymore: "I believe in God, the almighty, creator of heaven and earth. . . . " From then on, there are only passing references to God. We *address* ourselves to God but hardly say anything *about* God.

I think Buddhist metaphysics could be called the missing theology of God, the theology of Silence. You said earlier that it's mistaken to think that Zen Buddhism, or Buddhism in general, puts all the emphasis on the Silence or emptiness, not on the Word, on things, on the particular. That's obviously wrong, but there's something extremely valuable in the Buddhist approach to Silence, in Buddhism's focus on the Silence within the Word. The Word is Silence that has come to Word. When people forget that the true Word comes out of Silence and wants to lead us back into Silence, then conversation becomes chitchat and, more broadly, life becomes superficial. So the focus in Buddhism on the Silence within the Word seems extremely valuable to me. Buddhism unravels the silence about the Silence.

AR: There *is* a focus in Zen Buddhism on the silence within words. In one early text, a long poem called the *Cheng-tao-ke,*[7] we find the lines, "It speaks in silence, / In speech you hear

---

[7] *Song of Realizing the Way* (Jpn., Shōdōka), by the seventh-century Chinese Zen master Yung-chia Hsuan-chueh.

its silence." That is to say, the essential fact manifests itself in silence—and in speech as well. One salient way that the fact reveals itself in speech is in onomatopoeia, in such words as *buzz buzz* or *chop chop,* which present a sound directly. In Buddhism, we also have expressions known as turning words, which are direct presentations of the fact. They are the incisive point itself.

BD: Can you give us an example of a turning word?

AR: Of course. There'a well-known story of Ma-tsu and Pai-chang taking a walk and scaring up a wild duck. "What was that?" Ma-tsu asked.

Pai-chang said, "A wild duck."

"Where did it go?" probed Ma-tsu.

"It flew away," Pai-chang answered.

With that, Ma-tsu laid hold of Pai-chang's nose and gave it a twist. Pai-chang cried out in pain, and Ma-tsu said, "Why, where did it ever fly away?"[8] These are the turning words that located the true duck and awakened Pai-chang to it.

BD: It has a lot to do with what we said yesterday: we mustn't confuse reflexive thinking with living. Thinking is a second phase in which we reflect on living.

AR: Carried to the ultimate. And that ultimate is the realm of realization.

---

[8] *The Blue Cliff Record,* case 53.

⚄ 4 ⚄

The Two Traditions:
Differences, Intersections, Minglings

DIFFERING EMPHASES

AITKEN RŌSHI: Visiting Japan after World War II, I learned that Japanese people love to ask test questions—questions like "Who was the greatest American?" (When I answered "Henry David Thoreau," they were completely baffled, having obviously expected me to name George Washington or Abraham Lincoln or someone like that.) After hearing a number of these test questions, I developed some questions of my own, including "What do you think of Christianity?" Most replies went something like this: "Well, Christianity has taught us how to educate our young people. It's taught us how to take care of people through public health programs and through social welfare programs. But as to Christianity itself, I don't understand it."

It seems to me that there's a lot to be learned from that little story, about both Buddhism and Christianity. One thing it illustrates is that Buddhism has historically been weak in the social application of its doctrine and experience. In Japan and North Asia generally, it didn't give rise to the kinds of social service programs that we see in the West. It lacked an equivalent of the so-called social gospel.

There are many reasons for this, none of which probably explain it fully. To begin with, in India, Buddhism was an otherworldly path. When it moved to North Asia, it moved in on sufferance, in a culture where other religions were already well established and state power was strong. Buddhist leaders were told to be good boys, and it was made clear that Buddhism must support the royal house. For the most part, Buddhists confined themselves to monastic enclaves and were very leery of stepping outside the bounds that they felt were necessary to preserve the religion. As I say, that doesn't explain it completely.

In Christianity, on the other hand, the very teachings of Jesus demand that people who wish to be Christians take up the cross and follow their savior, which means to take up the cross of humankind and of the world, really. This is the way I understand it, at least. The unfortunate aspect of this great commitment to service is that it overshadowed the path to the profound religious experience that Jesus himself had and that undoubtedly was shared by many of his immediate successors. This path was not clearly enunciated.

BROTHER DAVID: When your Japanese friends said, "But as far as Christianity itself, we just don't understand it," I suspect they meant that they had never come in contact with Christian teachings. There's so much institution, so much activity, so much emphasis on education programs, and so on that even those who brought Christianity to Japan might have been very hard-pressed and totally stunned if you asked them suddenly, "What did Jesus teach?"

People of the Church don't often ask themselves what Jesus taught; we've mainly asked what we should teach *about* Jesus. I'm not saying that Christians have lived for two thousand years without knowing what Jesus taught; millions of people *were,* to some extent, in touch with his teachings. But his teachings definitely were not the focus. The focus of the Christian institution was on what we teach about Jesus, not on what Jesus taught about human life and God. How could the Japanese know what Christianity is, if for Christians themselves that question wasn't in focus?

A R : So there are genuine weaknesses in both traditions and genuine strengths in both as well.

B D : Do you have an idea of what Jesus taught, as distinguished from what the Church teaches *about* Jesus?

A R : Yes, "Love they neighbor as thyself." [Mk. 12:31]

B D : That's something that has been repeated millions of times throughout these two thousand years of Christian history, but that's the message of Jesus cut down to just a slice—a very important slice—of its moral teaching. It's also very significant that what most people, including most Christians, know about Jesus's teaching is the moral side.

A R : But this moral side is an ideal and a conviction that grew out of experience. The experience underlying "Love thy neighbor as thyself" has to be the experience that the other is no other than myself.

B D : That's right. Even in the strongly theistic culture in which Jesus lived and taught, mystics knew that the individual is one with all others and with God, but mainstream Christianity lost sight of the mystic tradition. That's another reason for the gap between Christianity and Zen.

A R : Isn't it even a little heretical in Christianity to say that God is no other than oneself? Wouldn't that be considered the ultimate in presumption?

B D : No, not at all. It's the ultimate in humility. The ultimate in presumption would be to say, "I am God." The ultimate in humility has been expressed very well in the little ditty by Piet Hein, "Who am I / to deny / that maybe / God is me?" When it's really boiled down to the essentials, that's close to both what Jesus taught and how he taught.

Jesus didn't go around saying, "Here is my message that I bring to you from God." He didn't speak like the prophets, who said, "Thus speaks the Lord." Instead, he taught with parables, asking "Who of you does not know this?" In other words, he placed the authority for his teaching in the hearts of his hearers. He rested his teaching on the divine authority, the ultimate authority, that spoke in the hearts of his hearers and that speaks in our own heart of hearts. "You know it already, don't you? Now act accordingly"—that's basically what the parable says to us. It catches us sort of admitting we know the truth already. Jesus' message and his teaching method were completely integrated.

AR: The idea that God is oneself was expressed in Buddhist terms by Hakuin Zenji: "This very body is the Buddha."[1]

BD: I think I understand what you're saying, but it would appear to some people when you put it this way that you're equating the terms "Buddha" and "God."

AR: No, not at all. Such a statement as "This very body is the Buddha" goes hand in hand with the essential message of the *Diamond Sutra*—that the Buddha is not the Buddha and so is called the Buddha. There is absolutely no concept, no archetype, no notion in Zen Buddhism that doesn't self-destruct, including "Buddha."

SAVIOR AND SAGE

BD: Maybe we should take the two terms *Savior* and *Buddha* and ask the pointed question, "To what extent is the Buddha a

---

[1] The line quoted is from his "Song of Zazen." See Chapter One, note 3.

savior and the savior Jesus Christ an enlightened one or Buddha?"

AR: In that same text I mentioned in regard to silence, the *Cheng-tao-ke,* the Buddha is referred to as the King of Doctors—in other words, the very best of doctors, one who can treat the ills of all beings. Along the same lines, among the various manifestations of the Buddha is one known as the Healing Buddha, who is always represented holding a vial of medicine. But the implication is that we must consult the King of Doctors for the treatment of our ills, not that the King of Doctors will come to us spontaneously. That may be one difference between the two types, savior and sage.

BD: It all hinges, of course, on the question of what saving means. Long ago, when I was first studying with Eidō Rōshi,[2] he made a distinction between two ways in which we use the word *saving.* On one hand, we speak about saving somebody who is drowning, pulling him out, saving his life. That's the kind of saving that most people have in mind when they speak about Jesus Christ as a savior. On the other hand, we commonly use the word in a different sense in phrases like *saving water* or *saving energy* and so forth. This means not wasting anything, or in positive terms, it means being keenly aware of the value of every drop of water, every bit of energy—affirming the value of these things.

In both senses, it seems to me, both the Buddha and Jesus are saviors. As enlighteners, teachers, they save us from error in the first sense: they pull us out of the illusions and misconceptions in which we're lost. In the case of Jesus, it's clear, if you look at the gospels—not at what we teach about Jesus but at his teaching—that he's also a savior in the second sense. The essential

---

[2] Contemporary Rinzai Zen teacher Eidō Shimano. Brother David began practicing Zen under his instruction when both were young monks. See reference to Tai Shimano in the Introduction.

point in his life, long before he dies on the cross, is that he affirms the value of every human being, very much to the distress of the authorities, who want to put those sinners and harlots and tax collectors down. He affirms the value of every human being as a human being and in that way saves them, by saving their self-respect, by making them stand on their own two feet and pulling them out of that consensus reality that their society had formed and that, sadly, hasn't changed very much in our society.

A R: The Buddha, of course, is you and me, and the first vow of the Four Vows, which Buddhists everywhere recite, is, "Though the many beings are numberless, I vow to save them." Literally, the words translate, "I vow to let them cross over," meaning to cross the river of suffering and to reach the shore of enlightenment. This is the Buddha's vow and our vow to transform all human beings, all beings, in fact, enabling them to reach what you would call the supernatural.

B D: So the process of saving, of enlightening or ferrying across, would be helping all creatures to come from what, to what?

A R: From a self-centered preoccupation with what Eliot in his *Preludes* called the "certain certainties"—"short square fingers stuffing pipes," death, sex, taxes, and so on. From this, we awaken to a recognition that reality is vast and boundless and has countless gates of entry.

B D: The way you've expressed it fits only the saving of human beings. How do you express it in terms of all beings, including spiders and African violets and so forth?

A R: In Hawai'i, there's no winter freeze to keep the lid on insect populations, so we have lots of bugs, and at our temples we've cultivated the practice of resolutely grabbing big cockroaches, carrying them to the door, and tossing them out, saying, "Be happy." I have one friend who, when he feels obliged to swat a cockroach, will say, "Better luck next time!"

BD: That's a way of saving the cockroach?

AR: Absolutely.

BD: With the well-wishing, in other words—the flow of energy toward it.

AR: Actually, it's very clear in Buddhism, except perhaps in the Pure Land School (and I can't speak for that part of the tradition), that all are saved from the beginning. The Buddha is said to have declared at the time of his great realization experience, "All beings are the Tathāgata," which is to say, all are enlightened, and he went on to say, "Only their delusions and preoccupations keep them from realizing that fact." So the King of Doctors takes it upon himself to remind us that we're limiting ourselves by our preoccupations. Lift those preoccupations, and you'll see that all beings are the Buddha.

BD: To spell out more fully what salvation means in a Christian context, we'd have to start where I started just a moment ago—by saying that Jesus saved people long before the cross was in view. He saved people by making them stand on their own two feet. That's how he was understood as a savior by his contemporaries. He gave them back their self-respect and gave them back their deepest relationship—to God, to the Ultimate—by reminding them that it was never lost. With Jesus, it wasn't, "Here, I give it to you." He never said, "I forgive your sins." Jesus says, "Your sins are forgiven," with the implied "Don't you know that?" It's his adversaries who said, "Who's that guy to forgive people's sins? Only God can forgive sins."

Of course, the authorities of his time—the political authorities, together with authoritian religious authorities—didn't look kindly on his saving people this way, just as their equals in Central America today don't look kindly on anyone who helps people stand on their own two feet. It's pretty obvious from the gospels, although one has to read them as late accounts of something that happened much earlier, that his saving activity was leading toward the cross and that Jesus willingly took this upon himself as a free, willing sacrifice for his cause, for what he stood for, and as a gesture of trusting God.

After he was put away by the establishment, his followers, although at first shattered and scattered, recognized that this kind of life can't be extinguished. That's what we call resurrection. It's presented to us in mythical imagery, and we can't unravel events to determine what happened historically—but that's not important for us. The important thing, clearly, is that he died and yet he lives. We can't verify that by going back two thousand years, but it is something that happens today in countless lives and can be experienced: he freed us. Christ lives in those who follow his path, and they live in him; that's the ultimate kind of salvation. They are alive with his life and, in turn, become saviors for others.

Today I never run into anybody who has great problems understanding that, but people do have tremendous problems with the concept "He died for our sins" as this has been taught in Sunday School. Jesus lived and died to end the alienation that we feel from our true self, from one another, and from the Ultimate Truth. He lived for this goal and had to die because he lived that way. In that sense, he died "for our sins." Unfortunately, over the course of the centuries, this has come to be presented in almost legal language, as if it were some sort of transaction, a deal with God: there was this gap between us and God, somebody had to make up for it—all that business. We can drop that. The legal metaphor seems to have helped other generations. Fine. Anything that helps is fine. But once it gets in the way, as it does today, we should drop it. We don't have to speak that language. We're free to present it in the way I have here.

AR: It's vividly clear from your account how the biography of Jesus has formed Christianity. It's equally true that the biography of the Buddha formed Buddhism, and we find parallels in the Buddha's life of Jesus' constant endeavor to set people on their own feet. But the great event of the Buddha's life took place at the outset of his teaching rather than at the end of his teaching, and the idea of a life directed ultimately to the cross is absent in Buddhism. In Christianity, the cross is sometimes called the tree, but it's a rather different tree from the Bodhi Tree, where the Buddha had his great awakening and which itself is identified with enlightenment.

I think that the directions that Jesus and the Buddha took were strongly influenced by their cultural environments, although they both rejected much of them. The Buddha grew up in an environment that was not monotheistic and in which the idea of vast, cyclical world systems—huge cycles of time and being—was commonplace; this context, as much as anything, opened the way for him and later Buddhists to evolve perhaps the most extraordinary metaphysics in all of the world religions, a metaphysics that it isn't confined to a single time line. I suspect similar cultural factors help explain why the Buddha's experience led to an emphasis upon enlightenment, whereas the life of Christ led to an emphasis upon salvation. These two words are weighted; they don't mean exactly the same thing.

CULTURAL ROOTS AND RELIGIOUS CHOICE

BD: I think we've already agreed that cultures or languages shape religious traditions and that, rather than spending our time trying to sort out the metaphors of our two traditions, we want to concentrate on matters of experience and practice. In that spirit, I wonder what you've found in yourself and in working with students whose cultural background is Western—in religious terms, mainly Jewish or Christian, I suppose—but who've chosen to practice an Asian religion?

AR: There are two kinds of people attracted to Buddhism in the West. The first group consists of people whose feeling for Western archetypes has faded to the point that the archetypes have become meaningless for them or almost meaningless. It's relatively easy for such people to adopt the archetypes of the new religion. They enter into that realm easily because the fading of archetypes from their own culture has created a vacuum in their psyches, a void that the seeker becomes quite eager to fill. This is often the case for a person who grows up in a family where there's very little religion or who becomes disillusioned with religion as a youth.

The second group consists of people—Catholics especially but also Jews, not so often Protestants—who want to remain within their own religion but who take up the methods and the archetypes of Buddhism to deepen and clarify their original religion, to become a better Christian or a better Jew. That was the purpose my own teacher, Yamada Rōshi, expressed for his work with Christians: he said, "I want to make them better Christians."[3]

B D: He couldn't have said that unless he recognized Christianity as a way that leads us to what's ultimately important. The goal is neither Buddhist nor Christian but rather, in the terms we've been developing here, the deepest human experience, explored continuously, lifelong, through practice.

This reminds me of the time I asked Thomas Merton whether he thought he could have presented the Christian teaching in the new or deeper or fuller way he did without his exposure to Buddhism. Usually, he just laughed off questions like that, not really answering them, but in this case, he became very quiet and said, "I'll have to think about that." Fifteen or twenty minutes later, after other conversations, he came back and said, "You know, I thought about your question, and I think I couldn't understand Christian teaching the way I do if it weren't in the light of Buddhism."

---

[3] Yamada Kōun was Aitken Rōshi's principal teacher and worked extensively with Christian Zen students. See the Introduction.

A R : Of course, the broad picture is not merely that some pilgrims are changing religions or finding, as Merton did, a benefit in studying other religions. The religions *themselves* are changing. Buddhism already has changed on moving to the West and will inevitably change more in years to come. I think a Japanese already would be a little surprised at the place that certain Asian archetypes occupy in the Western vision of Buddhism.

B D : Is that due to the encounter with other traditions?

A R : It's the acculturation of Buddhism in the West, the encounter of Buddhism with Western culture, which of course includes Christianity.

B D : As a participant in the last two decades of Buddhist-Christian dialogue, I've noticed an interesting change that may relate to what you're saying here. During the first decade, roughly speaking, the only people who really asked questions were the Christians. They asked burning questions, and the Buddhists were in the position of giving the answers. Now, at least as often as the Christians, the Buddhists ask the questions. I think that's a very interesting shift.

A R : I think it's reflective of the changes in Buddhism. These Buddhists now feel comfortable with their modified Buddhism and can begin to look for their own roots without being threatened.

B D : Going back to the question of practicing a religion that originated in another cultural context, I want to raise a question from Brother Kieran.[4] He accepts that our traditions issue from the same source and lead to the same area, that they're different but parallel and equally valid ways. Though he feels an affinity for Buddhism, this insight that the traditions are equally valid disinclines him from switching over to Buddhism because switching to it or any other religion would be saying, at least

---

[4] Brother Kieran O'Malley. See the Introduction.

implicitly, that the new one is more valid than the one left behind. I think that's a very interesting point.

Of course, one way out would be to say, "Yes, all these traditions are equally valid, but this one is more helpful to me."

AR: Where do I feel comfortable? With what do I feel deepest affinity? I think those are the bottom-line questions that the seeker needs to ask. Questions of equal validity or unequal validity can drop away.

BD: It's a personal thing, not an objective thing out there. For a very long time, Christians were obsessed with their uniqueness, the rightness of Christian faith and the errors of all other traditions. I think that was a kind of tribal mentality inherited from the Hebrew tribes and maintained in the Church until very recently—until the Second Vatican Council or later. But now, under the influence of people like Thomas Merton, millions of people have been influenced by traditions that are quite different. Conversely, at this point I imagine that there might be some Buddhists who would say they couldn't really understand Buddhism the way they do except for the light the Christian message sheds on it.

AR: I certainly find passages in the Bible that illuminate my understanding.

BD: You've done a great service, it seems to me, to Zen Buddhism in the West by drawing attention to the traditional Buddhist precepts, especially in your book *The Mind of Clover*.[5] As I understand it, the precepts usually don't get much attention in Zen, and your emphasis on this ethical element is extremely important, I think. To some extent, I imagine, this was a matter of redressing an imbalance that occurred in Zen Buddhism for social or historical reasons. But was it also occasioned in some way by the encounter with Christianity?

---

[5] *Mind of Clover: Essays in Zen Buddhist Ethics* (San Francisco: North Point Press, 1984).

AR: It couldn't have happened had I not grown up as a Christian. It would never have happened. There's nothing particularly Christian in that book, but because I grew up with that kind of worldview, I sought it in Buddhism and found it there.

Another thing comes to mind: you know, there wasn't a word for religion in Chinese or Japanese until the nineteenth century; the word was coined because it became clear that such a word was necessary in order to deal with Christianity. In Japanese, the word is *shūkyō,* and its literal meaning is "traditional teaching." You and some other Christians might consider "traditional teaching" a fit synonym for *religion,* but I think most Christians would choose other words, such as *faith* or *belief,* which express a more devotional attitude. I think Buddhists have something to learn from this approach. Thought of as "teachings," religion may be a bit dry. We Buddhists would do well to take our religion more to heart.

Buddhism is almost a matter of course in Japan. It's part of the culture, and I think most Japanese regard it as *merely* cultural. A temple is commonly considered little more than a place to make arrangements for a funeral and to conduct memorial services. I remember a survey taken in the early 1960s, in which students at Sendai University were asked, "How important is religion to your life?" They were given a choice of five answers, ranging from very important to not at all. I've forgotten the exact results, but an enormously high percentage of the students, maybe as high as 85 percent of them, said "not at all."

So it seems to me that Buddhism, as it develops in the West, will benefit from an injection of the more devotional religious attitude we find in Christianity. On the other hand, perhaps Christianity must shift toward an understanding that its own religion is a teaching.

BD: The pair of opposites I would use here are *static* and *dynamic*—the static and the dynamic aspects of the religion. Originally, every spiritual tradition is purely dynamic. The older it gets, the more static it becomes, and this solidification process begins very early. When we speak of Christianity, or of the "Christian tradition," it already sounds static, like something fixed. Originally, the Christians weren't even called Christians. It's a great event, recorded in the Acts of the Apostles, when they were called Christians for the first time. Though they were already pretty strong by that time, they had simply been called "followers of the Way." The great challenge I see before us is to make followers of the Way out of "Christians."

As long as we're "on the way," we're all followers of the Way. There's no great separation among people who are on the way, even if they follow different religious traditions. What matters is being on the way. We follow different paths in different garbs and different vehicles—that's the cultural part—but there's only one way of being on the way: to be on the move, *that's* the Way.

A R: A deep unity is apparent in the words and lives of great teachers. I've always felt that Meister Eckhart could shake hands with Chao-chou.

B D: There you're touching on a very important point. The great teachers of the different traditions, the ones who are accomplished by the standards of their own traditions, tend to understand one another very well despite cultural obstacles. The insistence on differences and the opposition to interreligious understanding comes not from the accomplished people but from those who are less accomplished. They prefer the static aspect over the dynamic, favoring this or that path over being on the way.

ℵ 5 ℤ

Keeping the Traditions Alive

THE DANGER—AND NECESSITY—
OF RELIGIOUS INSTITUTIONS

BROTHER DAVID: In the whole arena of religion and spirituality, I see institutions as a necessary evil. I put emphasis on both words: necessary and evil. I'm so clearly aware of the evil of institutions, even the best institutions, that I'm very reluctant to extend any institution's power or to establish an institution where one doesn't exist yet. But when I step back and try to look at this in a balanced way, I see institutions as serving life. That's their primary function, and they must always be adjusted, and at the right time discarded, for the sake of fulfilling it. It's *life* we should focus on and foster, always giving preference to life instead of the institutional structure.

The image I have in mind is that of buds in winter. As grade-school children, every spring, in February or early March, we brought branches of horse chestnuts into our classrooms. They have big, shiny buds, about the size of a child's thumb, and we'd watch as the buds gradually, gradually got bigger and then developed a few green lines. One day they would pop open, and out came the tiny, velvety hands of the horse chestnut leaves, and they unfolded, and the hard shell that had covered the buds just dropped off. Life does need these protective structures, but it also knows how to free itself continuously of them when they're no longer needed.

Institutions, unfortunately, rarely drop away when their usefulness ends. They have a tendency to be self-perpetuating and, often despite the best intentions, serve themselves rather than the life they were created to serve. That's why I say we ought to be extremely careful with them—to question authority continuously and to question our institutions—in order to make sure that the institution serves life rather than serving itself.

Of course, the degree to which institutionalization takes hold of a tradition can vary quite a bit. I've long admired the Zen Buddhist tradition for its ability to slither out from institutionalization and to free itself from the pernicious influence that an institution can have on tradition. Can you say something about that from your own experience?

AITKEN RŌSHI: I think it's true that in Zen Buddhism it's easier to slither out, but it's not always done. Senzaki Nyogen Sensei, my first teacher, was highly critical of what he called "Cathedral Zen"—of Zen institutions, particularly in Japan, that had become self-perpetuating, self-important, the center of justification, so to speak.

But yes, it's easier to slither out, and I think the reason is that the tradition has built into itself an understanding that institutions, rituals, priestly dress, and other such forms all belong to the sphere of metaphor. And metaphor, though it may join self and other in a most intimate way, is not itself the point.

BD: That understanding is built in?

AR: Absolutely, from the very beginning. This is the heart and soul of the *Diamond Sutra,* the heart and soul of kōan practice, the lifeblood of the teaching.

BD: Is there also an explicit awareness built into the tradition that the institution as such may be a necessary but very dangerous means to employ?

AR: Yes, I think so. We have wonderful examples of masters who walked away from their responsibilities as abbots of great temples and are revered for this. Ikkyū Zenji may be a good example. He was a fifteenth-century Japanese Zen master and renowned poet who felt there was a lot of hypocrisy in the big monasteries of his day. He's famous for turning his back on the institution and for criticizing it in his poems—not only institutional corruption in general but particular individuals.

One of the things Ikkyū Zenji criticized was maintaining the monastic pretense of chastity while, in fact, condoning sexual activity. He himself is a problematic model in this dimension, however, because he not only entered the houses of publicans and prostitutes, like Jesus, but probably patronized them as well.

BD: There are great figures in contemporary Christianity, too, who've stood far outside the Church as institution. One who comes to mind immediately is Steve Biko, who stood up for the rights of black South Africans. The churchgoing variety of Christian may have a hard time recognizing him as a saint, but he was as close a realization of what Jesus taught and stood for as anyone in our time—a great saint. An example from the Christian side that's closer to home is Martin Luther King, Jr.

In Christian tradition, there's also a built-in understanding, clearly evident in the way Jesus teaches, that what really matters is not the medium but the message.

In the Catholic context at this present moment in history, however, the institution has become so oppressive that it's, in large measure, counterproductive. Rather than facilitating the handing on of the message, it's making it more difficult.

AR: Although the Zen Buddhist hierarchy doesn't begin to compare with yours in the Roman Church, I don't want to create the impression that it has none. In Japan, the various subsects do have their hierarchies, with headquarter temples, then subtemples, and subtemples of the subtemples. Even so, people in those subtemples have a great measure of autonomy and select their own teachers, their own abbots. There's no such thing as abbots being assigned by the headquarter temples. The headquarter temples tend to be centers for propagation of the faith, so to speak. They receive scads of tourists, publish books, hold seminars, and the like.

The Sōtō Sect has the equivalent of two bishops, one at each of its two headquarter temples; the Rinzai Sect has none. Usually, a monk trains at a monastery no more than eight years, then goes out and is his own master at a smaller temple. A few stay on, either in custodian roles or because they show promise as future teachers, but the establishment tends to be dispersed rather than centralized, horizontal rather than pyramidal. In Western Zen, generally, it's even more so.

BD: The monastic movement within the Church (and I suppose this may be true of monastic movements elsewhere) is a deliberate effort to get out from under the institution, to get out from any labels, to free itself completely. The fact that monastic life often seems highly institutionalized is really an indictment of monastic life as we know it. As Thomas Merton said so clearly and so eloquently, the monk is a person without labels, a marginal person, a person out from under. The great challenge to the monastic community is to keep the institution in check and to make it serve life; the challenge for individual monks and nuns is to get away from preoccupation with the institution and to focus on life lived.

The only monastic model I've found that limits institutionalism in a very promising way is the Benedictine Camaldolese tradition. Here there are three poles of monastic life: in the center is the community life normally found in a monastery; to one side is the hermitage, where the monk stands on his or her own feet and isn't really under any institutional restrictions; on the other side is outreach, where the monk goes out into the extra-monastic world and again stands on his or her own two feet. In other words, built into the institution are two phases in which monks are largely unbound from the institution.

Now, that's the ideal. In the practical matter of carrying it out, there are still many problems, but at least it's an institutional structure that puts checks and balances on itself in a very healthy way, for the sake of life.

AR: To balance this discussion a little, I think we should acknowledge that one disadvantage of loose organization is that it provides few resources if trouble occurs. When all the various temples and training centers are independent, as they are in Western Zen Buddhism, there's no recognized authority to step in and help deal with problems. This disadvantage is felt especially when the problems are at the top, in the form of a rogue teacher.

TRADITION AND TRADITIONALISM

BD: Maybe we could relate this discussion to what I said earlier about religion's static and dynamic aspects. Institution, doctrine, ritual—these more or less static things are like a conduit within which the dynamic tradition flows. Sediment builds up in the conduit, unfortunately, and it may become so encrusted that nothing can flow through it anymore. We need continuously to encourage the dynamic aspect of religion and lighten the static aspect.

It may seem contradictory to speak, as I just did, of a "dynamic tradition." As it's usually understood, the term *tradition* would seem to belong to the static side of things, to refer more to the conduit. But *tradition* really means "the process of handing on," which is an active thing. Christians tend to think of the tradition being handed on as a fixed entity, like a dowry. But a tradition changes as it's passed. The challenge is to be faithful to tradition without falling victim to traditionalism.

AR: Lately, I've been reading the letters of Gerard Manley Hopkins,[1] so I'm reminded of a comment he made to his friend and fellow poet Robert Bridges: "The effect of studying masterpieces is to make me admire and do otherwise." In other words, we should find inspiration from tradition but not imitate it, be loyal to tradition while making our own way.

BD: There's all the difference in the world between being rooted in tradition and being stuck in tradition. You can't tell offhand, at certain times and in certain seasons, whether a person or a particular community is stuck or rooted in tradition, just as you can't tell, when the leaves have dropped, whether this little thing sticking out of the ground is a seedling that's rooted or a lifeless twig that somebody's stuck in. You have to wait for the spring. When springtime comes, we'll see whether it puts forth leaves or whether it doesn't put forth anything and is just stuck.

If it puts forth any leaves, of course, they'll be new leaves— basically the same sort of leaves other plants of this kind had in the past but new, in a real sense, and different in details. Admire the past and do otherwise, as you just quoted Hopkins. That's the great challenge for any tradition: to always bring forth something that's brand new and yet in some sense the same. The downfall of every tradition is the ritualization of what was originally alive.

AR: As Thich Nhat Hanh says, "Every act is a rite."[2] There's great virtue in the rite; we just have to avoid making it into a fixed ritual.

---

[1] Nineteenth-century British Jesuit priest now known best for his poetry. The quotation is from *Gerard Manley Hopkins: Poems and Prose,* selected and with an introduction and notes by W. H. Gardner (Baltimore: Penguin Books, 1963), p. xxiv.

[2] Thich Nhat Hanh: a contemporary Vietnamese Buddhist teacher who lives in exile in France and has a large following in the West. The phrase quoted is from *The Miracle of Mindfulness* (Boston: Beacon, 1986), one of his numerous books.

BD: The question is, what's the difference between a rite and a ritualistic ritual? Or even between a good ritual and a ritualistic ritual? I'd suggest that ritual, in itself, is a very positive thing that springs naturally from our deepest experience because we want to celebrate that experience and to celebrate it in a great variety of forms. Every way of celebrating it that appeals to our feelings, our sense of beauty and so forth is really ritual in that sense. But when ritual hardens, loses its connection with that original experience and becomes a reality unto itself, something to be repeated out of some inner or outer compulsion, then it's ritualistic. That's not to say that repetition itself makes an act ritualistic. As long as the umbilical cord, so to speak, between the deep experience and the ritual isn't broken, the ritual is nourishing and nourished.

AR: In Zen Buddhism, we have a ritual of bowing to the floor, known as *raihai*. Commonly one does raihai before the image of the Buddha—not *to* the Buddha but *before* the Buddha. One evening at the beginning of the Gulf War, we had a meeting to share our feelings about the attack, and a profound feeling of intimacy grew up among the people who were present. At the close of the gathering, we recited our vows, as we customarily do, and after that, ordinarily, would come raihai before the Buddha. This time, on the spur of the moment I said, "Let's do raihai to each other." So we all bowed in a ring to each other. It was a kind of spontaneous rite, celebrating our unity—not only the unity of the group but the unity of all beings.

BD: That's an example of a ritual that's alive and therefore can be modified.

AR: Played with, yes. In that connection, I think of Sōen Rōshi,[3] a great ritual master, forever making innovations. I call him the Balanchine of Zen because he was always choreographing peo-

---

[3] Nakagawa Sōen, late master of Ryūtaku Monastery and teacher of both Aitken Rōshi and Brother David. See the Introduction.

ple. At the drop of a hat, he could turn having a cup of coffee into a coffee ceremony, modeled on the tea ceremony, with all its rich ritual. He could take a group of giggly middle-school girls visiting his temple on a field trip and choreograph them so that they were taking delight in temple rituals such as sitting in meditation and reciting sutras. He did it just by acting it out with them, making a joke out of it if somebody wasn't standing up straight and so on. The children ended up loving it and loving him. Unfortunately, many of his monks didn't like him. They thought he was peculiar, heretical.

BD: I think their contemporaries thought that about many great teachers. They certainly thought that about Jesus.

PART TWO

Everyday Practice

≈ 6 ≈

Practice with a Capital P

PRACTICE AND PRACTICES

BROTHER DAVID: You speak as a householder, and I speak as a monk, but what we're discussing here applies quite equally to householders and monks. Whether one lives in a private home or in a monastery shouldn't make much difference in terms of practice.

AITKEN RŌSHI: I agree, though the historical Buddha seems to have considered it impossible for a householder to attain the highest and the best. Indeed, a synonym for *monk* in the Buddha's time—and even today, in some Asian languages—is the term *home-leaver*. Buddhism incorporated the probably pre-Buddhist idea that the duty of a householder is to practice moral living, so that he or she may accumulate sufficient virtue to become a monk or a nun in a future rebirth. This concept, with the resulting division of monks from laypeople, persists today in Buddhist countries both in North Asia, where the Mahāyāna and Vajrayāna traditions predominate, and in the southern tradition of the Theravāda. An increasingly vigorous lay Buddhism has developed, especially since the Kamakura Reformation of the thirteenth century, but many Asian Buddhists still maintain a sharp, and fundamentally incorrect, distinction between laypeople and the ordained.

I tell my students that our duty is to find the way to leave home without leaving home—in other words, to find the way of practice within our households. This is a major challenge because Zen practice, in its formal aspect, is very rigorous and takes a lot of time and usually does involve a degree of physical separation from the household. No one can do zazen easily in a room full of children. How to work this out is an ongoing problem, one we discuss often. We're always seeking ways to involve young parents and small children, and most turn out to be inadequate. So when we speak about practice, although in one sense it's the same thing for monks and laypeople, there *is* a whole dimension of practice that's special.

BD: I'd call that dimension *practices,* to distinguish it from practice singular. Practices are designed to help you in your practice. Everything depends on making these practices work in one's given situation, be it monastic or domestic, so as to build practice in its totality. The misunderstanding too easily creeps in that prayer and the vows and so forth are where it's really at, while the impatience you feel when you take your children to school or the arguments you have with your friend, lover, or spouse—that this is somewhere beyond the margin of the spiritual life, sort of a derailment from the proper track of prayer and meditation. We must avoid putting too much emphasis on practices, which are a means to an end. The end is practice, our whole lives as practice.

AR: Practices are means to an end, and at the same time, as Dōgen Zenji said, they are the end itself.

BD: How do you understand that? I can understand it in the sense that practice is everything we do and suffer. Obviously, in that aspect, the practices are part of the practice. Everything we do is an end.

AR: Yes, and the other side of that very general statement is that, through such practices as, say, zazen, we're able to discover real zazen, real practice. Unless there are particular practices, there is no practice.

BD: I understand. I think I can parallel that in Christian terminology by drawing a distinction between prayer and prayers, a distinction I've often found it necessary to make. Everything we do should be prayer, in the sense of communion with divine reality. Brushing your teeth ought to be prayer. In this sense, *prayer* is another word for practice—practice with a capital *P,* if you want. Prayer is supposed to go on at all times, even when we're sleeping. In this sense, prayers aren't the plural of *prayer* but are a means to that end. Prayers include meditation and other such methods, time set aside for nothing but communication with the Ultimate.

AR: So if it's communication with the Ultimate, then there are no means and no ends at all. Practice is not a means.

BD: No, it's an end in itself. But when it comes to prayers as a means to an end, namely prayers as a means to the prayerfulness that should go on at all times, what you've said is true: unless you have prayers, unless you set time aside for nothing but prayer, you won't have prayerful living. When you look at it in this context, you can say—and it sometimes shocks Christians when I do say it—that the person of prayer, the true pray-er, is not distinguished by the amount of time that she or he devotes to saying prayers or doing meditation but rather by efficient use of prayer time. True people of prayer need to say fewer prayers than others because their life *itself* is prayer, is practice. There's a misconception that the more time you spend saying prayers or doing meditation, the better. My contention is, the less you need, the better.

AR: I think that both are true: the less one needs, the better—and we need a lot of prayer to reach that place.

BD: I would agree. But to say that one needs a lot of prayer to get there is simply a realistic assessment, quite different from falling into the trap of thinking that prayers are really the essential thing rather than a means to an end.

I like to draw an analogy between food and prayers or practices. You don't assess the cow by how much hay she eats but rather by how much milk she gives. The best cow is the one that needs the least hay and gives the most milk, not the one that eats the most hay. Likewise, the religious life properly should be assessed not by the number of hours we spend in specific activities such as praying or meditating but by our way of being.

AR: I think that we can usefully distinguish between training—the formal elements of Zen training, such as zazen and dokusan—and the totality of practice. Training is part of practice. Practice includes training. Without training, in my view, practice would be incomplete. But training alone isn't the way of religion at all.

BD: That's so important! I think the word *practice* has been narrowed in many circles to mean simply sitting on your cushions. If we limit our practice to training, it isn't really what we mean by practice.

AR: No, it's a hobby or a kind of cult activity.

BD: Formal training is *practicing* practice, so to speak.

AR: How can we encourage people to practice in the sense we intend?

BD: The first answer must be: by again and again bringing them back to their own experience of something that goes far beyond what they now realize.

AR: Also, it seems to me that the Buddha and the Christ encouraged people to practice by their own examples. Maybe they didn't need to preach a single sermon.

BD: That's true, but I don't want to stop there. More important than just doing his own thing and thereby being a good example is that the Christ awakened other people to the fact that they had it in themselves. That's the decisive thing. If you become aware—and this is something that I have to remind myself of over and over again—you can do it. There *is* a way. Trust this power within. Then you can move beyond the limits that you set yourself and that you resign yourself to. It's crucial to remind people that they have this capacity—that experience of the Ultimate and the deepest kind of practice are available to each of us.

Practice "Off the Cushions"

AR: Perhaps this is the place to look at what practice is when one is off one's meditation cushions. It's attention, it seems to me. It's mindfulness, not in the sense of constantly evaluating what we're doing but rather in the sense of giving full, rigorous attention. In communicating with others, attention is love. If you speak with your eyes lowered or if you're looking out the window, there's a lapse in love there.

BD: So this attention or unreflective mindfulness that you consider the essence of practice is really love. One could also say that prayer is mindfulness, that prayerful living is mindful living, again meaning mindful in the unreflective way you indicated. Anyone who's really fully mindful will realize that everything is a gift. Nobody owes it to us, we haven't bought it, we haven't paid for it. It's gratuitous, and our response to this gratuitous reality is gratefulness. That's really the essence of practice, and that's where we meet.

This connects with learning to listen, not only learning to listen to sounds or to other people but, in the widest sense, to listen to the message that comes across, moment by moment, from the universe. On that level, I think it helps to notice at least one surprise each day—something that's surprising, unforeseen. It may be the weather; it may be a sight that catches one's attention; it may be a pleasant event or even an unpleasant one. By opening our hearts to something surprising, we begin to see how many surprises there are every day, and we begin to see that we live in a universe that, in some way or other, talks to us. Once we recognize that, it's quite natural to listen because we want to hear what the message is.

AR: I agree. My only question is about the distinction you've made between the sounds of things or people and the sound of the universe. I don't think I've heard the sound of the universe. What we're hearing is the sound of the thrush or the sound of the wind in the trees or the sound of the stream here at Waipi'o. We can say that it's the universe speaking through the bird or the winds, but I find that a bit abstract.

BD: Yes, I agree. But on the other hand, there's a level of attention to the song of the thrush that includes an awareness that what you hear is not just this particular thrush—that in this particular thrush you really hear the voice of the universe or the voice of the earth.

I'll give you an example. In his *Sonnets to Orpheus,* Rilke has a poem about a fountain of the kind you find in Italy, one with human figures and streams of water gushing from their mouths into the basin below. He describes looking at it, aware of the long way the water has come—out of the spring, through the aqueducts—before finally coming out of this mouth and going back into the earth. As he listens to the splash the water makes in the basin, he says, it sounds to him like a monologue of earth. The decisive lines are:

> ... Only to herself
> Does earth talk this way. When a pitcher is inserted,
> It seems to her that you have interrupted her.

To me, that dimension of the great sound of the universe, in whatever you hear, is valuable and inspiring.

AR: Can there be two inspirations here?

BD: Do you mean the inspiration of the universal and the inspiration of the particular? Yes, definitely—enhancing one another.

AR: To me, the inspiration is when the entire universe disappears, and there's only the song of the thrush sitting here in this chair.

EVERYDAY ASCETICISM

BD: In the context of everyday practice, it may be important to say something about asceticism. I don't mean a monastic asceticism but just making a place for self-denial. *Asceticism* literally means "training," like an athlete's training, and broadly refers to setting an order that will be helpful in making progress in the spiritual life—training yourself by clearly and deliberately ordering your times and ways of sleeping, eating, dressing, sexuality, entertainment, and so forth. It's very difficult to carve out a place for training of this sort in our society. It goes against the grain of our society.

AR: Of course, at a Zen monastery or during sesshin in a lay temple like ours, that place of training is created for us. For example, you learn not to swing your arms when walking around the grounds or, if you're a monk, when walking anywhere. There are many such strictures to support the training.

BD: Most of these practices, like not swinging your arms or placing your sandals parallel when you take them off, the right one on the right side, the left on the left—they're all meant to make you mindful. That mindfulness is the important thing; the actual content of the practices is secondary, at best. Accepting these little strictures and working faithfully with them enables us to become mindful and also expresses again and again our dedication to changing ourselves. It reaffirms this dedication at least to oneself and maybe to others, though that's less important. The willingness to change and to show it in small matters is a very important element of practice.

AR: I agree. It's one of the things that distinguishes someone who's practicing from someone who isn't.

BD: The asceticism we're urging, of course, is rather different from asceticism as it's usually understood. In Christian tradition, there's often been a negative attitude toward the good things in life, toward sensuousness and so forth—a suppression of a sense of beauty, of pleasure, of saying yes to life. Of course, this tendency wasn't genuinely Christian, nor was it universal; it isn't found in the Benedictine tradition, for instance, which is fully life-affirming and grateful. To a large degree, though, this suppressive attitude prevailed in the Church.

Now the pendulum has swung over in the other direction, and it's very clear to the best of the young monks who come to the monastery that, in order to find the fullness of life they're looking for, they have to cultivate not only a life of prayer but also their talents at pursuits ranging from music to poetry to film appreciation or even to good, wholesome cooking. What's very difficult for them to see is that there's any room to deny oneself anything. They think that's just compulsiveness. I don't want to destroy this enthusiasm for life; on the contrary, I want to heighten it. But I think we need a balance between this appreciation of the sensuous and appreciation of what can be learned by setting limits. I'm not talking just about monks. This applies to anybody who decides to strive seriously in spiritual life.

AR: In each individual who takes up the life of practice, there's a creative tension between self-indulgence and asceticism. We must continually challenge ourselves to find the middle way. And as I'm fond of saying, the middle way isn't merely a midpoint between extremes, a compromise; it's really the creative way rising out of the tension.

All too often, asceticism produces rather awful compromises rather than creative resolutions of the tension. In Zen monasteries, there's a simple vegetarian diet that all the monks follow rigorously, but when they step outside the monastery walls, they eat fish and meat and drink beer like anybody else—more than anybody else, in fact, to make up. In the temple where I trained, they had a "secret" monthly feast at a nearby farmers' shelter, a shelter the farmers had erected for themselves where they could go to wait out a heavy rain. The monks would crowd in there and cook up all sorts of food that wasn't allowed under the monastic regimen, and the abbot wasn't supposed to know about it. Of course, having trained there as a monk himself, he knew all about it. Also, once a year they'd have a wild party, with great drinking, lascivious dancing, and so on.

All this was in keeping with Japanese character, which includes a full and positive recognition of the body and its functions and its needs. The problem is that they tried to practice a strict asceticism 90 percent of the time and then acknowledge their body and its needs the other 10 percent, dropping the ascetic element entirely.

BD: The Christian tradition attempted (with rare instances of success) to develop an asceticism best expressed by one of the Desert Fathers in a story from the fifth or sixth century. The key phrase is learning to be "masters of the body, not slayers of the body." That's the idea: to be masters of the body, playing on the body as though on a fine instrument.

Asceticism is rightly understood as life-enhancing. Saint Bernard, one of the great masters of monastic asceticism, wrote a book about fasting in which he lists its benefits. The first benefit of fasting he names is that after fasting one appreciates the taste of food much more. That's ascetic. It's *not* life-denying. It's life-enhancing—enhancing life by restrictions, by setting limits.

This fact seems to be lost even on people who are otherwise serious and dedicated, so, as I said, within the Christian tradition the pendulum tends to swing nowadays from a very unhealthy self-denial to an unhealthy self-indulgence. Will you say something, from your experience, about self-fulfillment through self-denial?

AR: This goes back to what we said earlier about the self, about experiencing ourselves as the multicentered self. A person who's realized herself or himself as the great multicentered self—not just intellectually but through a deep experience—will naturally tend to practice what you're calling "self-denial." It's self-denial only from the perspective of the limited self. From the perspective of the multicentered self, it's really self-fulfillment. In touch with the multicentered self, we feel pleasure in finding ways to reuse paper that has print on one side, to conserve gasoline, and so on. We find self-fulfillment as the multicentered self.

Bashō has a haiku that relates to all this:

> Journeying through the world,
> To and fro, to and fro,
> Cultivating a small field.

This haiku brings to mind the Amish, who feel that an eighth-grade education is enough, that a few acres of land are enough, that tools of intermediate technology are enough. Within these limits they are free, at least the most mature of them are free, to find fulfillment in what they achieve and the way they live. Narrow and deep. The opposite pole is represented by the Renaissance person of many accomplishments and many interests. Who's to say which of these people is happier?

BD: I'd like to find a guiding principle that applies equally to the fulfilled Amish farmer and the fulfilled Renaissance person. It will have to be an objective principle yet also take into consideration individual differences—one's talents, shortcomings, and so forth. Perhaps we can borrow a guideline on poverty established by Hubert van Zeller, a Benedictine writer whose books about the spiritual life were popular in the middle part of this century. He wrote, "If you can do without it, do without it." Rightly understood, that's an objective principle, but it also includes the personal element in saying "If *you* can do without it. . . ." Another person might not be able to do without it.

Applying this principle requires a great deal of clarity. One has to be clear that there are many things we *think* we can't do without but can, in fact, do without very nicely. Far more important for me is the other side: there are things people suppose they can do without and really can't. Among them are the beauty and poetry of daily living. This goes back to the old interpretation of asceticism that drained it of so much vitality. We humans can't do without beauty.

AR: What's the nature of those things I might want but can do without? They're the things that will enhance and aggrandize my self-image.

BD: Not the multicentered self but the other, little self.

AR: That's right. On the other hand, the things I want to do without but really need are things that enhance the multicentered self, that enhance my self as the Buddha.

BD: I think that's well expressed. It complements the statement "If you can do without it, do without it." It also points out that a guiding principle like this needs to be very carefully studied and interpreted.

AR: Yes, we can't be simplistic about this matter of desires, of attachment and nonattachment. In the late 1960s and early 1970s, there was a lot of glib talk about non-attachment. Katsuki Sekida, a dedicated layman who came from Japan to live at our temples in those days, brought it home to me very clearly that a person who's not attached is not alive. An absolutist position of nonattachment—nonattachment to food, nonattachment to shelter—means death. Less literally, nonattachment to friends and music and good books means a kind of inner death.

ℵ 7 ℤ

The Transformation of Character

REFINEMENT AND FORMATION

AITKEN RŌSHI: In Buddhism, there's the realization that all the elements that make up the self are empty, essentially empty—that there is no self to begin with, you might say, or that the self, as it is, is empty. The expectation in Zen is that this realization will be constantly reinforced by practice and that thereby Zen students will become selfless, in the other sense of the word—ready to give themselves freely. There are no built-in structures to ensure that this process will take place, however. In this area, I think we Buddhists must enlarge ourselves by taking inspiration from the Christian way.

BROTHER DAVID: What you call the Christian way is really quite universally practiced in healthy cultures. Living with you for these days, I see that you've built into your own life certain elements of this natural, healthy discipline. For instance, your not eating between meals would typically be something that, at first, demands a certain self-restraint. How do you look at it?

AR: I feel it's disorderly to eat between meals.

BD: But you obviously think that not eating between meals helps your practice.

AR: Yes, it *is* my practice, and it's almost unconscious.

BD: By now. That's the type of thing I'm thinking about—a certain refinement (as opposed to crudeness) in the way one lives. Do you think that such refinement is important to practice, or is it irrelevant?

AR: I think it's quite important. Refinement comes with attention. A person who behaves crudely is a person who isn't paying attention to his or her impact on other people or on the environment.

BD: That context of attention makes the connection with practice. Unfortunately, monks sometimes display real crudeness in behavior, table manners, dress, and so on. Of course one can't generalize; there are many outstanding opposite examples. What bothers me is that a lot of the monks who lack such refinement would say, "What does that have to do with holiness?"

AR: It has everything to do with holiness! In the *Five Modes of Honor and Virtue,* a classical formulation of Zen by the great Chinese master Tung-shan, you'll find the line, "For whom do you bathe and make yourself presentable?" If this very body is the Buddha, then I honor the Buddha by making myself presentable. Doing so expresses respect for myself as the Buddha.

BD: That ties in beautifully with ancient guidelines for Christian hermits, who were told, "When you eat, don't just pick up some food and eat. Fix yourself a meal, set the table, put a flower on it and a candle maybe, as if you were receiving a guest. Then eat your meal, wash your dishes, and clean up nicely, not in a sloppy way." But where do you draw the line between good manners that are merely a social convention and good manners as an expression of a refined heart?

AR: It seems to me that it depends on where the behavior comes from. Is it real or artificial? Does it come from a loving heart or only from wanting to be accepted? Usually, it's transparently clear which is which. You can read it in a person's body language. I think in this regard of my teacher, Yamada Rōshi. No one could be more gracious. He always remembered to thank me for even the littlest thing that I did for him and would go out of his way, even if he himself weren't feeling well, to ask how I was feeling.

This reminds me of the importance placed on nobility in the earliest Buddhist teachings.

BD: *Nobility* meaning what?

AR: Meaning a kind of nobility that has nothing to do with the invidious sort of social stratification that we find in every society (and probably in every monastery and in every zendo). The word *noble* was used to indicate the excellence and virtue of the way, as in the names given to some of the Buddha's core teachings—the Four Noble Truths and the Eightfold Noble Path. A commoner, socially speaking, could be noble in this sense. Yamada Rōshi said, "I wish to become like a great tree, shading all beings." It's that kind of nobility, I think, that Zen students should hold out as the ideal. Unfortunately, not all students reach this level.

This takes me back to my initial question: a Buddhist center has a body of rules that shapes communal life and supports the practice, but when I referred to built-in structures, I was thinking of the formation training found in certain parts of the Christian tradition. There's no equivalent in modern Zen. Would you say a little bit about this process of formation?

BD: In the strict sense, formation is the process by which one is trained within a religious order or community, but it may also include a layperson's work with his or her spiritual guide. We speak of ongoing formation, recognizing that it's a lifelong process.

AR: It's really a directed process of character change, isn't it?

BD: That's what it's meant to be. It entails a complete readiness to be changed. Would that willingness to change be part of Zen training?

AR: Yes, I think so, but the actual process of change isn't as clearly formulated in Zen training as in the Christian tradition. This parallels the different treatment of morality we find in the two religions—the great stress placed upon it in Christian practice and the all-too-light attention usually given it in Buddhist practice, at least in Japanese Buddhist practice. In Japan, from earliest times, the precepts haven't been taken seriously. In the Zen context, the precepts are treated as kōan material, as instruments of realization that are then to be embodied in one's life. But how these precepts are embodied is left almost wholly to the students themselves, and they tend to take their moral guidelines from Confucianism and Shinto rather than from Buddhism.

Whatever process of formation there is in a Zen monastery is incidental, almost casual. I've heard more than one abbot use the image of a rock tumbler as a metaphor for the beneficial effect that life in the monastery has on a monk's character: in the ordinary life of the monastery, people are thrown together over a long period of time, rubbing against each other, so to speak, and polishing their characters in the process, as stones in a tumbler become smooth by rubbing against one another. That's as far as the tradition of formation goes in Zen. It's not formalized a bit.

BD: In Christian tradition, the process is less often considered under the term *change* than under the term *transformation,* as in Dietrich von Hildebrandt's excellent, though now somewhat outdated, book *Transformation in Christ.* At the beginning of the book, von Hildebrandt makes the important point that, when we commit ourselves to the process of transformation, we shouldn't suppose only our negative aspects will be corrected.

That part is pretty obvious. What's less readily apparent is that *everything* will be transformed, particularly one's good side.

AR: Yamada Rōshi said, "The practice of Zen is the perfection of character," but he never elaborated on that. Feeling a need to flesh it out, I've been giving talks lately on the perfections, the *pāramitās,* a classical Buddhist formulation of human virtue. I'd like eventually to develop a little book specifically directed toward inner questioning, like the Christian manuals of character formation, taking up one of the perfections each month, say, and listing questions for each.

BD: It's unfortunate that, at this point in history, when Buddhism in the West is discovering the importance of such things and seeing certain models in the Christian tradition that could be useful, the Christian tradition itself has largely lost confidence in those models. Today, formation in Catholic communities is nothing to brag about. Many of the people heading our communities were subjected in the course of their own formation to unreasonable, narrow, dry, dead interpretations of asceticism and obedience and so forth. Some of them were injured, actually, and so have rejected the process of information as they knew it, while lacking anything positive to offer in its place. Maybe Buddhists and Christians can reinvent the formation process together.

DEMONS INTO DAIMONS

BD: The Greek word *daimon* means "divider," and it eventually got the meaning of *demon,* a person or a spirit that divides people, causing strife by setting one against another. But originally daimon had no such negative connotation. It refered to dividing things in the ordinary sense of distributing them, of parceling them out. You can see how the negative sense may have grown from the positive.

In practice, we reverse this, turning our demons, our evil inclinations, into positive characteristics. Demons are just forces that have been misdirected. How do we go about turning them into creative, constructive forces? The first and probably most important step is to recognize them as destructive, but from then on, what do you do?

AR: Suppose one's demon is an imperative to power. When I look back, I realize that my most promising students have felt this imperative. It was a terrible problem for them in the beginning; they were resented in the sangha rather strongly because others felt dominated, but with time, this turned around. The immature imperative for power, it seems to me, is mixed with the imperative to prove oneself. With practice and the coming of maturity, there's no longer anything to prove, yet the positive potential for power remains.

In other words, the imperative to power may be transformed into what the Japanese call *toku* and the Chinese call *te,* as in the title *Tao Te Ching,* which Arthur Waley translated as *The Way and Its Power.* The word is ambiguous, signifying not only power but also virtue, so when Paul Carus published a version of the *Tao Te Ching,* he called it *The Canon of Reason and Virtue.* This is the quality that leaders in traditional societies gradually acquire through good conduct and wise decisions. With character change that includes the confidence of inner peace, power can be the power of Gandhi or Martin Luther King or Jesus or the Buddha.

BD: Actually, in English, *virtue* also means both power and a firm disposition to do good. *Virtus,* which stands behind it, may mean a disposition to do good either in the moral sense or in another way. For instance, the virtue of a plant might be its power to heal or its beauty. So there's a perfect parallel between the Chinese and the English.

As for converting the demon of the will to power into a daimon, I'd say that power that manifests itself demonically is demonic only because it springs from thinking that there isn't enough to go around; thus it divides and leads to strife. That same power can be a power of service, of distribution, when coupled with the deep inner peace in which one is fully aware that there's enough for everybody; thus things may be distributed instead of grasped.

This applies equally, I think, to other sorts of demons. So the basic way to turn your demon into a daimon would be to go back to that place of piece.

AR: And practice. Practice itself enlarges the dimension of peace.

THOROUGHGOING TRANSFORMATION

AR: There's a story frequently told in Japanese Zen circles about a man from a Rinzai Sect of Zen who came to do zazen in a temple of the Sōtō Sect. In the Rinzai school, people are seated facing the center of the room, while in the Sōtō school, people sit facing the wall. This fellow seated himself in Rinzai fashion, facing into the room, removed his glasses and put them down in front of him, got himself comfortably settled, and began to do zazen. Just as he was entering deep *samādhi,* the monitor came along, tapped him on the shoulder, and instructed him to sit facing the wall.[1] So he turned around and faced the wall. As he sat, he felt he'd never been so focused, never so deeply centered, never achieved such a profound peace. When the bell was rung to end the period, he swung around for *kinhin,* stood up, stepped on his glasses, and suddenly found himself cursing loudly![2] So much for his samādhi.

I tell that story by way of illustrating how easy it is to fool

---

[1] *Samādhi:* Sanskrit term for meditative absorption.
[2] *Kinhin:* formal walking meditation, usually practiced between periods of zazen.

oneself about one's condition. It also shows the relative nature of samādhi. This sort of relative settling can occur, but it's very different from the peace, tranquility, and groundedness that one enters by real experience of emptiness and oneness.

BD: Are you then saying that the experience that this man had wasn't a real experience of peace, even though he thought it was?

AR: That's right. He had temporarily quieted his mind, but it was just a kind of extreme point in the ordinary swings of mental condition between quiet and noisy.

BD: Right. By implication, you're also saying that even though we may feel we've reached this deep peace, we can't be sure until it's tested in practice.

AR: You bet. The proof of the pudding is in the eating.

BD: As you say, it's awfully easy to deceive oneself about one's practice, motives, and character. Can one "undeceive" oneself?

AR: I think there's a streak of self-deception in everyone. If the historical Buddha hadn't had a streak of self-deception, he wouldn't have needed to go through his long training. If Jesus hadn't had a streak of self-deception, he wouldn't have needed to spend forty days in the wilderness being tempted. The crucial thing is to confront our self-deception, to find a way to isolate it and look it squarely in the eye, the way Jesus did.

BD: Really, the ultimate temptation is always self-deception. You may remember that in *Murder in the Cathedral,* T. S. Eliot's play about Thomas à Becket, three agents of temptation appear, representing the ordinary temptations of power and so forth. After that, a fourth appears, and Becket is astonished. He says, "I expected three. Why is there a fourth?" The fourth proves to be himself. He overcomes his self-deception in the end with the famous lines, "The last temptation is the greatest treason: / to do the right deed for the wrong reason." That's really the ultimate temptation and the ultimate self-deception. How do you get over that? By yourself?

A R: It seems to me that one doesn't get over it alone. The other might speak to you in a vision or a dream, or it might speak to you in the form of your spouse or friend or teacher. In teaching, I use the expression *holding up the mirror,* telling people—and telling myself, too—that it's our responsibility to hold up the mirror for one another, to say, "Look, this is how you're coming across to others. Don't deceive yourself." I want people to hold up the mirror in that way for me, too.

B D: So you do need the other, but you need that kind of other who is so deeply rooted in the common ground or whatever one chooses to call it—the Sacred Heart, the space under the tree—that it's your true self you see when the mirror is held up. You encounter your true self in another. When that happens, the "undeceiving" can happen. Of course, neither this nor other kinds of character change occur swiftly.

A R: As it happens gradually, gradually, over a period of many years. People close to you may not even notice the increments of change, but it's happening all along and late in life, if all goes well, brings a kind of second childhood in the best sense of the word—that childhood in which, Jesus says, one enters the kingdom of heaven. In this regard, I think of Father Lassalle.[3] I have a photograph taken when he was eighty-five years old, in which his face seems to be the face of a child.

B D: There's a book with four photographs of him on the back—one when he's about six, one when he's in his twenties, one when he's in his forties or fifties, and one when he's in advanced age. In his eighties, he looked almost exactly the way he looked as a little child! But what do you make of this phenomenon?

---

[3] Roman Catholic priest Enomiya Lassalle, now deceased, studied Zen in Japan for many years.

AR: Certainly, our true life resides in the very simple. Thich Nhat Hanh says if you can't explain something about Buddhism so that a child could understand, then it isn't worth explaining. There's a long, intermediate period in our practice when this isn't true, when a student of religion may need explanations too complicated for a child, but the fundamental things are all latent in the child's heart and can always be appealed to. We cultivate them throughout our lives, bringing them to full flower in our late maturity, it seems to me.

BD: Even though, as you said, it takes a long time, during that time we cultivate this child continuously within. Among the qualities that we cultivate are trust and immediacy, intimate contact with the world, and so forth. Those are the positive aspects, but there are negative qualities in childhood, too. What's the difference between being childlike and being childish?

AR: I think of the famous passage in First Corinthians [1 Cor. 13;11]: "When I was a child, I thought as a child. Now that I am an adult, I put away childish things."

BD: That touches on the decisive point. As adults, we have to add to the great qualities of children one quality that they lack—responsibility. If responsibility is missing, we'll be childish. If we have it, we can't be childlike enough.

AR: You've put your finger right on it. A childish person is a person who evades needs and obligations, who cannot respond appropriately to them.

BD: One aspect of the child that's appealing is its immediate response to things, but in a child, this is just responsiveness, not responsibility. That isn't demanded of a child. As adults grow into second childhood, we, too, ought to be able to respond to things immediately—to respond with a child's directness to beauty, tragedy, need—and to do so with a sense of responsibility. If we fail to recognize our responsibility and to make the necessary effort, then we wind up being merely childish.

Ease with Oneself

PRACTICING PERFECTION

BROTHER DAVID: Like many earnest practitioners, I'm a perfectionist. Coping with this tendency has been a lifelong struggle for me, though it's less of a struggle now than in the past. I've come to my own way of working with this, but I want to ask how you advise people who are stuck in this trap.

AITKEN RŌSHI: I'm reminded of a conversation I had with Yamada Rōshi with respect to a person who was studying with both of us. I said, "I think that student tends to be perfectionistic," and he answered, "Well, I think it's wonderful to try to be perfect." I thought about that for a long time and viewed his words in terms of the pāramitās, the six Buddhist perfections—charity, virtuous conduct, forbearance, energy in moral development, focused meditation, and wisdom. Perfection of any of these virtues is a perfection of them all.

It's interesting that perfection can refer to a process—the process of perfecting one's playing of a piece of music, say, or perfecting a certain shot in tennis. In this sense, it really means making something better and better, not actually achieving an absolute state of perfectness. The word *practice* is similar. An attorney practices law, and a doctor practices medicine. That means that the attorney or doctor is doing it, not doing it in order to get somewhere but just doing it. Grasping this dual meaning of the term, we can move forward in our perfections.

BD: Very helpful. This would mean, for instance, that I could say to myself, as a perfectionist, "Don't focus on reaching perfection. Focus on perfectly *striving* for it."

AR: It's a lesson all of us need to learn. As children, we tend to be perfectionistic: "I want to do it exactly right." One responsibility of parents is to assure children that their best efforts are fine, that Grandma doesn't really care if your letter has lines that go uphill. We're in process of always getting better. If its parents don't help a child understand this, the child will grow up feeling, "That's too difficult for me, so I'm not going to even try. I can't do it well, so I'm not going to do it."

BD: I think most of us have both kinds of experiences—parents or teachers who demand perfection and leave us feeling discouraged and others who are encouraging, demanding no more perfection than the perfection of perfect striving. The latter are really our greatest help, for there's no denying that at every step we come across the imperfections of reality.

My way of dealing with reality's imperfection is to come to a breakthrough that I can only express this way: reality simply has to be perfect. Nothing less will do. But the moment it's at least perfectly *im*perfect, I can accept it. This isn't a play on words; it's not a little trick I'm putting over on myself. It's my way of expressing the anguish I have to deal with every day and the breakthrough that frees me from it.

AR: This breakthrough, as you call it, is fundamental to realization: all things are fine, essentially fine, just as they are. This isn't in any way a denial of my own faults or of poverty and war and the other horrors of the world, though literalists will tend to read it that way.

BD: In one sense, we must learn to be "comfortable with ourselves," but to what extent? Being too comfortable with oneself leads to complacency. How do you draw the line here?

AR: I'd put it this way: I'm not yet as I should be, according to my own vision of myself. If I can be comfortable with that, then I've found the way, the middle way.

BD: What you're saying implies two elements: one, recognizing the imperfection for what it is, with the implication that you'll try to overcome it, and two, accepting it, for the time being, as where you are.

AR: It also implies accepting my life as a life of practice and being comfortable with that. Practice always carries the implication of "Not yet, not enough yet."

BD: Process is the key word, as you mentioned earlier—perfection as process. In Christian tradition, we've made the mistake for a long time of viewing perfection as something static, thinking that the unchangeable is really perfect, that change isn't compatible with perfection. But that is absolutely not true. In music, in dance, and in our own maturation, the perfection lies in the change, lies in the process. In our daily life and our daily practice, we have to gain an appreciation of the not-yet as an aspect of perfection.

COMPETITIVENESS

BD: I personally don't have a competitive mind at all. In fact, when I was a boy, teachers wrote in my report cards that a more competitive spirit would be highly desirable. There's one quality usually associated with competitiveness that I highly value, however: the drive for excellence. As a perfectionist, obviously I value excellence. It's the light side of my shadow, the virtue of my vice.

I have the idea that maybe, in our educational system and in our spiritual striving, we could take from the competitive attitude what's good—the striving for excellence—and leave the rest behind. If striving for excellence is understood as an excelling not of the other but an excelling of your own best up to that point, then a little competitiveness may be for the best.

AR: Even in the religious sphere, an apparently competitive situation actually may be conducive to excellence. On my first visit to Ryutakuji, a monk asked me in Japanese, "Have you gone in to fight with the rōshi yet?" That was temple slang for having an interview, and indeed, when we look at dialogues between Zen teacher and Zen student or between two Zen students or between two Zen teachers, superficially it may look like competition, but what's really happening is that they're striking sparks together, something that couldn't happen if only one were present or if they didn't have this intense, head-to-head encounter. Each is functioning at his or her own peak of excellence, challenging the other to do better, and this may carry one or both of them to realizations they couldn't have achieved alone.

BD: That's usually called "dharma combat." Isn't it a misleading term?

AR: Only as misleading as my friend's question about fighting with the rōshi. An exact translation of the original Japanese word, *hōsen,* would be "dharma battle" or "dharma war." Taken literally, of course, it's misleading, but they're using *sen* (war, battle, combat) in a specialized way, as so many words in both the Buddhist and the Christian traditions are used.

BD: Yes, we have such terms as *spiritual warfare* in Christian tradition, and I'd like to abandon them. They're not merely words. A whole image is conjured up, and it's an imagery very prevalent in our society and very destructive. The challenge I see before us right now, before you and me at this moment, is to find an imagery to replace that of the battle, a more accurate imagery. What comes to mind, though it's not yet what I'm looking for, is the image of a training partner. In running, in track, sometimes one has a friend or comrade run alongside, not to compete with you but to push you, encourage you.

A R: But that relationship is unequal. The relationship in the dokusan room or in the public situation of so-called dharma combat, is most often unequal on the surface (because usually one party is the teacher and the other the student), but in terms of the dialogue, it's equal. Both are struggling to express directly and subtly the way things are.

But I agree that there are dangers in such terms and images and even in the public dialogue itself. I don't use the term *dharma combat* myself, preferring the less loaded word *shōsan,* which literally means "small work," as contrasted with the big work, *daisan,* of private dialogue between teacher and student. I feel ambivalent about the ceremony itself, however, because it tends to arouse the pathological kind of competition that you've been alluding to and that I, too, want to avoid. People feel regretful that they didn't do better in that public setting, in front of their friends and fellow students. Or else they feel proud that they did well or jealous that somebody else did well or mad at themselves because they didn't have the nerve to get out there and try it. I see the advantages when it works, but it often doesn't.

B D: I still wonder if another image wouldn't reduce or remove this pathological kind of competition, as you put it. For instance, when musicians play a duet, rather than trying to defeat one another, each tries to play better and better, challenging and inspiring the other to play better and better, so that together they'll make beautiful music. We could also use an image from the theater. We speak of actors upstaging one another; that's the competitiveness we want to avoid. When two excellent actors co-star, they build each other up, raising the level of each other's performance.

AR: Right! And they don't merely build one another up, but they build the drama up. That's the point. This is what happens in a real encounter in Zen practice, either in public or in the privacy of the dokusan room: they build the *Dharma* up.[1] The two individuals disappear.

BD: In other words, challenge is the essence of it. Not in the sense of one knight challenging another to a duel but in the sense of challenging each other to meet this situation excellently.

AR: That's the initial impetus, the challenge, but the real point is the encounter.

BD: And the encounter is meeting a situation the best way you can.

AR: Exactly. And the way you do that is to stand on your own feet and not be drawn in by the other.

BD: Is there something here that ennobles or maybe even rescues competition? Or is this the opposite of competition? Maybe we can say that competitive situations arouse powers that are, in themselves, desirable such as the impetus to surpass yourself. These should be cultivated and fostered, but competition as such should be discouraged.

In working with a small group of people on a project, if I see competitiveness springing up, I say, "Wait a moment. We're not like kids who are playing a game of marbles in which one has to lose marbles in order for the other one to gain marbles. This is a different game. We're like kids building a sandcastle where the marbles will roll down from the top in little channels, sort

---

[1] *Dharma:* Sanskrit word meaning "law" (natural, governmental, or religious) or phenomenon. In this case, it refers to the Buddhist law, i.e. the wisdom of the Buddhas.

of like a roller coaster. Let's build it together." I try to remove the aspect of competition.

AR: How about a situation in which two people are selflessly bringing forth quite radically different, conflicting ideas about what to do for the good of the institution? I don't know whether to call that competition or encounter or what, but surely that process of thesis and antithesis can lead to a good synthesis.

BD: Right. The competitiveness comes in only if the ideas are held selfishly: "That is *his* idea, and this is *my* idea." Then if one wins, the other loses. So I'd make an effort to depersonalize the ideas by saying, "We have different ideas of how best to proceed. We all contribute our best while respecting other's contributions." We want a win-win situation serving the project or institution rather than a win-lose situation serving the individuals.

The Ability to Say "I Don't Know"

BD: Among the many things that profoundly impress me about the Dalai Lama, quite high up on the list is his ability to say, "I just don't know." I've often wished that other people in prominent positions wouldn't feel the compulsion to have an answer for everything and would feel equally free to say, "I don't know." It's a sign of wisdom to know that you don't know and a sign of stupidity to think you have to know everything. I admire it enormously in him, and I wonder why so few people in leading positions reach that stage.

AR: The anxiety to have a ready answer, it seems to me, has two aspects. One is "I want to be equal to this question." Especially for someone in a position of leadership, for someone who's expected to have answers, not having an answer is equated with failure. We want our knowledge, our sense of the world, to form a reasonably complete pattern, one that will hold up under questioning. The second aspect of the problem is that it's very difficult for most people even to find the quietness that is the mind of "I don't know." Their inner monologues go on and on, constantly, so in response to a question, out comes that inner monologue, just projected into public discourse.

In the *Book of Serenity,* there's a famous story of the monk Fa-yen visiting Ti-tsang, his uncle in the Dharma lineage.[2] Ti-tsang asked, "What is your journey?"

Fa-yen said, "Going around on pilgrimage."

"What do you expect from pilgrimage?" Ti-tsang inquired.

"I don't know," answered Fa-yen.

Ti-tsang said, "Not knowing is most intimate." With this, Fa-yen had his great realization.

Not knowing is most intimate. Intimacy, as I said earlier, is realization itself. When you are intimate with something, you are one with it. When the Dalai Lama says, "I don't know," he's showing himself and showing the truth.

BD: That helps. The actual experience of unity, of being one with an object or an action or a person, is a knowing from within, as it were. This is quite different from the way in which we normally know, namely reflexively. You know reflexively only when part of you steps back and reflects on an experience.

AR: After the fact.

BD: In the dynamism of the doing, there is no reflexive knowing.

AR: So when the Buddha had his great experience under the Bodhi Tree, he simply looked up and saw the morning star. That was his great realization, and *then* he said, "Now I see

---

[2] Case 20 of the *Book of Serenity (Ts'ung-jung-lu),* a Chinese Zen classic of the twelfth century. See Thomas Cleary's English translation (Hudson, NY: Lindisfarne Press, 1990). "Uncle in the Dharma lineage:" Fa-yen's teacher and Ti-tsang both received authorization to teach from the same master.

that all beings are the Buddha." First the experience, then the reflection of experience in thought, words, actions.

BD: So to say "I don't know" may be far more than a statement of ignorance. It may be a statement of being in life, being part of it, being one with it.

AR: It may be, but it isn't necessarily. In any case, though, acknowledging openly that we don't know something requires real confidence—that comfortableness with ourselves and with our imperfection we spoke of earlier.

VANITY AND SELF-RESPECT

BD: What about vanity? Is a little vanity so bad? I'm thinking of a teenager who typically has a comb sticking out of his back pocket and is perpetually arranging the lock of hair on his forehead or something like that. These little vanities. Maybe one should consider them part of a necessary condition or stage on the road to maturity, one that comes at different ages for different people. What occurs to most people in their teens might occur to others, perhaps as a kind of repeat phase, in their thirties, forties, or fifties. If we see it that way, then it's vital to be extremely patient with them and their vanities.

AR: When I was a counselor at a juvenile hall for a brief period long ago, I was struck by the boys' concern about their personal appearances. They were forever shining their shoes, forever pressing thier blue jeans and their blue prison work shirts. I didn't get the impression of vanity, though, from those boys. I felt that I was seeing a struggle for self-respect. I think we need to see vanity sympathetically in that light, as a perhaps inappropriately directed effort for self-respect. A person who goes around looking like a slob may not have much self-respect.

BD: There's a parallel to competition here, I think: the bright side of competition is striving for excellence. The dark side of competition is putting others down. The dark side of vanity or pride is also putting the other person down. As long as you don't put another down, there's nothing wrong with putting yourself up.

AR: Or putting yourself in a presentable manner. Of course, what appears to be vanity may really be a symptom of self-consciousness.

BD: True. And what do you say to someone afflicted with self-consciousness? To tell someone not to be self-conscious only tends to increase self-consciousness.

AR: Obviously, you *don't* say not to be self-conscious. It's like the old story about telling a person not to think about a hippopotamus; he or she will find it hard to think anything but hippopotamus, hippopotamus. No, steer someone who's self-conscious toward practices that decrease self-consciousness, without even discussing the topic. Encourage such people to devote themselves to each task, forget themselves in each task. Yamada Rōshi said that "The practice of Zen is forgetting the self in the act of uniting with something." There is no self-consciousness in true practice.

At the same time, we should acknowledge here that self-consciousness isn't bad; in its place, really, it's very good. But when self-consciousness takes over, then the individual is paralyzed.

BD: Yes, when it blocks us. That's normally what we call self-consciousness.

AR: In psychoanalytic terms, it's an abnormal subservience to the superego. This relates to our need for a strong sense of the self.

BD: In what sense?

AR: We need a strong sense of "who I am" before we can let go of ourselves, of our self-images and self-concerns. My example of a person with a weak ego is the guy who walks into a bar, and the bartender greets him, "How are you today?" and the guy says, "Gee, why do you ask me that? Do I look sick or something?" Unless you can say, "I'm fine, how are you?" you're not really ready to start your practice. You have to feel, to a certain extent, "I'm really all right."

BD: I remember once befriending a young man, who said to me suddenly, almost shocked at making this discovery, "What are you doing? You're building up my ego. I'm trying to get rid of my ego." I answered him, "I have to build it up first because you have no ego to let go of." That was many years ago and has stuck very clearly in my mind. It's more or less what you've just said.

AR: Exactly. This isn't a black-and-white matter, not the only factor in the practice equation, but I find that those who have a strong sense of self often step most easily through a realization experience. Then they need to practice moderating this sense of ego because it all too easily becomes spiritual pride or what Chögyam Trungpa called "spiritual materialism."[3]

BD: Of course, spiritual pride takes many different forms, often very subtle, and it's very tricky to deal with, especially in a situation where it's a plain fact that one person does a certain thing better than others. For example, let's say that someone has come closer to right livelihood than others. To look at that and face it is at least a temptation to self-righteousness. I think people who are very sensitive to keeping their integrity often are a little taken aback when they notice that in this or that respect they really do better than others.

The only thing I can suggest in such a case is that one cultivate gratefulness. If I get closer to realizing my own ideals than someone else does, it isn't primarily through my own merit; rather, it's a gift. It's been given to me, and I focus on that aspect: Where would I be if I hadn't had this teacher, this upbringing, these friends, and so forth? I might be far worse.

---

[3] Chögyam Trungpa: the late teacher of Tibetan Buddhism and founder of the Naropa Institute in Boulder, Colorado. See his *Cutting through Spiritual Materialism* (Berkeley: Shambhala, 1973).

I think it's good to be able to make a clear and honest assessment, to be able to acknowledge to oneself that, on a particular point, I may have moved a bit further along the road that someone else. But we must remember not only that we owe this to the chances we've been given and the help we've received but also that along other stretches of the road we're lagging far behind. In other words, it's important to be able to acknowledge our weaknesses as well as our strengths.

AR: The first problem is even to glimpse our own pride. It's difficult to notice except upon reflection. I find that sometimes a little instance of pride will surface as I'm falling off to sleep, and I'll realize, "Oh, I tended to brag a little bit there."

BD: How do we distinguish between a pride that's negative and a just pride, pride taken in a genuine and worthy accomplishment? I'm thinking of those young men in juvenile hall who kept their clothes clean as a matter of self-respect. On the one hand, pride comes very close to self-respect, and that's positive. On the other hand, if pride entails putting down someone else, praising oneself at the expense of someone else, that's negative. Again, it may come down to a certain sense of competition. If pride is free of competitiveness, it's simply self-respect or a fair assesment of the situation.

AR: Pride, in the negative sense, is feeling "holier than thou."

BD: It's not just competitiveness but really comparison that's at the heart of the problem. "Comparisons are odious," as we say. In the last analysis, no two people or situations are directly comparable; we're all different people with totally different backgrounds. In this light, I have to take back, at least partly, what I said about the acknowledgment that one is farther along the road than someone else. If you remove that comparison, then wrongful pride will collapse of itself.

AR: If you're fully at ease with yourself, then any comparison is beside the point.

≈ 9 ≈

Issues at the Heart of Practice

RECKONING WITH FEAR

BROTHER DAVID: What do you tell your students about fear and faith? Is fear compatible with faith?

AITKEN RŌSHI: Yes, I think so. In the face of fear, especially the deep fear that we encounter in "the dark night of the soul," we may feel we're in danger of losing our faith, but with encouragement and support from spiritual friends and from a good teacher, we can stay on course. We stay on course with the faith that this fear, which includes (but isn't limited to) fear of losing our faith, is truly part of the path. I think that almost every true student of a religious way goes through a crisis of faith. It's just part of the process, and so long as the student is well read in the religious literature, she or he can understand it as actually an encouraging step: "I'm moving through the same crisis as my betters before me, so I'll proceed, even though it's very dark and I'm full of fear."

BD: Of course, ordinary fear would be a different matter. If you travel a very dangerous mountain road, it's appropriate to feel fear because then you'll drive more carefully. That's an appropriate fear, but we're not talking about that. We're talking about existential fear, and if I understood you correctly, you regard that sort of fear as compatible with faith, though opposed to it. In other words, the two belong together and are experienced together, as a polarity; they belong together in that sense, as opposites.

I remember that in a talk he once gave, Suzuki Rōshi explicitly spoke about this existential fear and faith in Buddhism.[1] What he said was completely applicable to the notion of faith in the Christian tradition: "It's all right to have that fear, as long as your faith stays a nose's length ahead—then the more fear, the greater the faith."

But maybe we should clarify our terms before going further. Is the notion of faith in Buddhism different from that in Christianity? Are we talking about the same faith?

AR: One of the requisites of good Zen practice, according to traditional Rinzai Zen teaching, is great faith, but this isn't a faith in something, certainly not a faith in a god or gods.

BD: That's a big difference, most Christians would say. But I've studied the question carefully and have found that the original meaning of faith in the Christian as well as the Buddhist tradition is trust, not beliefs. Most Christians say *faith* and mean *beliefs*. Certainly, beliefs relate to faith, but we mustn't confuse the two. In Buddhism, there's little emphasis on beliefs, is there?

AR: Beliefs clearly are relative; they have no fundamental basis. Fundamentally, on the original ground, there's nothing to believe in.

BD: This nothing is much more difficult to believe in than something—anything.

---

[1] Shunryū Suzuki, late abbot of San Francisco Zen Center, was among Brother David's teachers. See the Introduction.

AR: "Nothing" sounds like something when you say it that way! Let's be clear about this: I'm not talking about something that Zen people just *call* "nothing" or "the void" or "emptiness." I really mean *nothing.*

BD: Can you convey the sense of faith in Buddhism without referring to the notion of beliefs?

AR: Earlier I quoted Hakuin Zenji's statement "This very body is the Buddha." Whatever your vocabulary might be, however you might express it, this is the key point of faith.

BD: That's a belief, really. Not that I have any objection to it, but what you've stated could fairly be called a belief.

AR: Unless a student has some intuition of the truth of the fact that this very body is the Buddha, then you're quite right: it's a belief, and any confidence he or she derives from it will be hollow. In other words, you can't suppose that "this very body is the Buddha" is true because Hakuin said it; rather, in some way you must *experience* that it's true.

BD: I think the key word, which slipped into your last answer, is *confidence.* That's obviously how you understand faith, as confidence. Linguistically, it's just another form of faith, con-fid-ence. That f-i-d is the Latin for *faith,* so *confidence* actually is an intensive form of the word *faith.* Faith, when you try to speak about it without direct reference to beliefs, can only be confidence or trust, existential trust. In this sense, Christian and Buddhist ideas of faith coincide. Faith is the experience of confidence, ultimate confidence—courageous trust in life, you could say, if you want.

AR: Confidence in nothing whatsoever.

BD: That, of course, isn't the way Christians would put it.

AR: Confidence that even the abyss is really all right.

BD: That statement does have parallels in Christian tradition. For instance, C. S. Lewis speaks about God in the context of faith as an abyss of silence, into which you can throw your thoughts forever and never hear an echo.[2] That's our act of faith: you throw yourself into it.

But I hear you sort of sighing, and I think I know why—because this image comes from a totally different direction. That's true, but as we've already agreed, all religions are exploring the same existential ground, so it's natural that Christians, speaking our particular language, will make discoveries similar to those Buddhists have made. You don't seem convinced. I agree that Zen Buddhism has a much more direct, immediate, expressive, and focused method to confront students with that abyss than Christianity has. As we agreed at the outset of these conversations, however, the various traditions are really only so many ways of becoming fully human, and in the quest to become fully human, I think, people in all traditions reach this abyss of faith and will have at least somewhat similar experiences there.

AR: It seems to me we've been walking around a crucial point for a few days here: inevitably, the way that we express the ultimate colors the ultimate.

BD: And it colors our practice, and that's why this is so important for us.

AR: It colors our practice, too, yes. These are differences we should respect and maybe even celebrate rather than gloss over.

PAIN AND SUFFERING

BD: I suppose all seekers wish there were a painless release from suffering. Would you agree that there's no such thing?

AR: Yes. Yamada Rōshi used to say, "Pain in the legs is the taste of Zen"—a natural quality of the process, in other words. In

---

[2] Lewis, best known as a novelist, was also a highly respected lay theologian.

general, if zazen periods are of reasonable duration (we suggest no longer than twenty-five minutes) and if allowances are made for those whose legs are bad, the light-to-moderate pain one will go through in zazen can actually be helpful. It can be the physical dimension of the "dark night of the soul," which one must go through anyway. The dark night, of course, itself is a painful psychic and emotional experience, and in some cases, it takes physical form as bad health, in extreme cases such bad health that one literally dies.

BD: Or at least goes through a life-and-death crisis.

AR: In many Western Zen centers, pain is artificially induced, and this plays into popular American expressions such as "When the going gets tough, the tough get going" and "No pain, no gain." There's too much of this in Zen, I think. Even in the writings of D. T. Suzuki, whom I regard with great fondness and respect, you find the notion that in Zen your path must be blocked at every turn until, out of sheer desperation, you will break through the barriers. I find this imagery, and the attitude behind it, very unfortunate. Really, all obstacles must *dissolve* before one can settle in that space under the tree, and these obstacles are organic to the person involved. The warrior imagery of breaking through and so forth must be employed very carefully. Like other metaphors, it's useful, but it's important not to push the metaphor too far or interpret it too strictly. Perhaps I allow the pendulum to swing a little too far in the other direction, but that's the risk I'd rather take.

BD: In the Christian tradition, these metaphors have also been ridden very, very hard. I want to join you in going on record as being utterly opposed to the artificial creation of pain. There's enough pain in the world without artificially inducing any.

On the subject of natural barriers, I think of the second of the *Four Quartets,* in the section on the wounded surgeon, where T. S. Eliot speaks of "the absolute paternal care / That will not leave us, but prevents us everywhere." He uses the word *prevent* in a double sense—the usual, modern sense of posing an obstacle but also the old, early sense of being there ahead of us, getting there ahead of us and preparing the way. In doing so, he treats the question of pain in a very healthy way, it seems to me. In the Bible, the image almost universally associated with pain is of birth pangs—an experience of an impasse and, at the same time, a breakthrough.

AR: "The whole universe groaneth and travaileth until now." [Rom. 8:22]

BD: Exactly. That's one of many passages in which this metaphor occurs. So my answer here would be that, whenever we experience pain, it's a signal of a challenge, of danger. If it's serious pain, it's an invitation to wake up to the insight that a new birth is demanded of us. That makes this pain a growing pain that will lead us into greater maturity. I think that's a very positive aspect of pain.

AR: That's very instructive for me, and I acknowledge its truth. I guess the next question is how to handle the pain, how to work with it. As you say, pain signals a new challenge, and this is positive, but for the time being, it's painful! Any kind of shock demands recovery, so one shouldn't be perfectionistic and suppose we ought to be unfazed by pain. We may even need to withdraw a bit, temporarily. That gives you the space to heal.

BD: If I understand you correctly, you're suggesting that a certain withdrawal may be needed for the sake of going through with it, for gaining strength to push through. I have nothing to add to that.

AR: Of course, there's a kind of withdrawal that amounts to running away. That's different and counterproductive.

BD: We don't want to encourage that. We want to give people encouragement to get all the space they need to go *through* it.

THE PAIN OF THE WORLD

BD: I've run into quite a number of people who express blindness to the problems around them. "Everything's crumbling around me," they say, "but I don't see what the problem is." We've already referred to an unwillingness to face one's own pain, and it seems to me this is just another form or expression of that. In this case, I think, not seeing is simply a consequence of not wanting to see, probably a not wanting to see so deepseated that they really aren't aware that they're blocking their own vision. They just can't see it. Do you run into this?

AR: I acknowledge a possible problem here, as you say, in people who block themselves from being open to others. But there's also the phenomenon of a tragedy that takes the most open person by surprise—when a friend commits suicide or a business folds, and you really had no inkling such a thing might happen. There are times when feelings like those you report are justified: "Things are falling apart, and I didn't have any inkling they might be falling apart." Maybe that can't be changed. In any case, it's important to help people be more aware of the suffering of others and more willing to take it in as their own.

BD: While you were talking, the answer to my own question occurred to me, I think for the first time. Nobody wants to suffer, either directly, themselves, or by opening to the pain of others. Everybody wants to have joy and life. If we encourage people to be more alive—to find the area of their enthusiasm and feed that area—then they may gain in vitality and then be able also to take in stride the pain and suffering that's part of life.

AR: We can certainly encourage people who are closed down around their pain to feel that they're all right, so that they aren't constantly protecting themselves from their own pain. If I encounter such students, I try to find a way to assure them that I share their pain.

BD: But the best thing you do for the student, I'm convinced, is nothing you say but just the attitude you project, by which you radiate the message, "You're okay." When I'm with you, I get that message very strongly, so you're doing what you said just now.

AR: With occasional lapses.

BD: We'll make allowance for that! As you say, it's good to acknowledge that the pain is shared, not something that only unenlightened people or highly emotional people feel. Have you seen the T-shirts that say, "Suffering is optional"?

AR: It's not true! Only by putting ourselves in a stupor of some sort could we, in our day, cut ourselves off from suffering—and that's just another kind of suffering.

Let's look at the word *suffer* here for a moment. "To experience pain" is only its secondary meaning. Its primary meaning is to *allow,* to permit. Jesus says, "Suffer the little children to come unto me," meaning to let them come. To suffer illness, really, is to allow illness. People turn it around because they don't want to be ill. They're resisting illness and maybe making themselves worse. Suffering is really life itself. We're permitting life itself. We're allowing it.

BD: That's very beautiful. To put it another way, there are two ways of suffering: with the grain of life and against the grain. To suffer with the grain of life is also to suffer, is also painful, but it's growing pain and it's life-giving. To set yourself against the flow of life is suffering against the grain and is fruitless. It's important to see this difference and set ourselves into suffering with life. Etymologically, *suffer* means "to bear from below" *(sub-ferre).* It implies supporting, carrying.

I once attended an audience with His Holiness the Dalai Lama where he was asked about the difference between Buddhist and Western approaches to suffering. It was one of several questions put to him by Westerners viewing their own cultural heritage in a very negative way, questions that built up Buddhism at the expense of the Christian or larger Biblical tradition: "Your Holiness, Buddhism has taught this wonderful way of overcoming suffering. What do you have to say to those Western traditions that have been wallowing in suffering for two thousand years?" I feel some sympathy for this question because, as I've said, I myself think that pain and suffering are overemphasized in the Christian tradition; it's quite an unhealthy streak there.

I was touched by the way the Dalai Lama answered this and other pejorative questions, being very careful not to claim a superior position for the East. I can't quote his response verbatim, but it was so important to me that I practically learned it by heart. First he said something like, "Now, wait a moment, wait a moment," toning the question down. Then he said, "In Buddhism itself, suffering is not overcome by leaving pain behind. Suffering is overcome by bearing pain for the sake of others." That's the bodhisattva ideal, and in my opinion, that's the last word that can be said on pain by Christians or anybody.

AR: Bearing pain for the sake of others. How about "bearing pain *with* others"?

BD: With others. With others who aren't even "others."

AR: That's right!

DISCOURAGEMENT AND PATIENCE

BD: It's easy to get discouraged both about our practice and about the state of the world. Sometimes we even get discouraged about being discouraged!

AR: Yes, that awful, sinking feeling: "Good heavens. There I go again. I've blown it. I've made too sharp a response again." At worst, I think, it's a discouragement one feels at recognizing a pathological, or at least negative, tendency in oneself and not knowing how to break out of it. It's a feeling of being stuck in or circumscribed by onself: "How can I not be angry? How can I not be depressed?"

G. K. Chesterton said that the reason angels can fly is because they take themselves so lightly, and surely laughter therapy can help here, just as Norman Cousins has shown us that it can actually cure cancer, for goodness' sake. But I think it's very difficult to break the cycle of discouragement by oneself. I think you don't need a shoulder to cry on as much as you need a friend who'll stick a pin into your bubble of despair.

BD: Or at least into your rear end! I think being brought out of oneself, as you suggest, can be very helpful in escaping discouragement. But I also think we need to cultivate an attitude of patience. How does one learn patience?

AR: This is an interesting one. The Chinese character for *patience* is made up of two elements. One means *sword,* and the other means *heart.* So it's the sword over the heart. How do you conduct yourself when there's a sword over your heart?

Commentaries on the pāramitā, the perfection, of patience (or endurance) list ten kinds of patience, ranging from the excruciating kind of endurance that's implied by the etymology of the Chinese word to the profound patience that's based on an acknowledgment that everything is empty. To put this deepest form of patience in more personal terms, it's a patience grounded in the place that doesn't move, the place of true equanimity. From this place, we can say, "Never mind. It won't matter at all a hundred years from now."

BD: I use devotional objects to foster patience, just as the beads of a rosary are devotional tools to foster mindfulness. My tools to cultivate patience are fossils that friends have given me. I have a small trilobite, an ancient marine animal, and another that may be an early form of the nautilus, and recently I received a tiny fish that's six hundred million years old. I look at those and handle them, and that's helpful to me. You just mentioned a hundred years from now. Imagine six hundred million years from now!

I also think of Hopkins's sonnet on patience, which ends with the words, "He is patient. Patience fills / His crisp combs, and that comes those ways we know."

AR: The comb, of course, is the honeycomb, and we know the ways that the honeycomb is filled—bit by tiny bit, by thousands of bees.

BD: And *that's* practice. Rilke also has a passage that fits perfectly and illuminates another aspect of patience. Speaking of the human condition in general, he says, "Like busy bees, we gather the nectar of the visible into the great golden honeycomb of the invisible." We gather the multiform world into emptiness. The honeycomb must be empty before honey can be gathered in. So from the fullness into the emptiness, to gather this sweetness—that's our task. All we need to add is that this process is as slow and as drop-by-drop as the gathering of nectar by bees.

ℵ 10 ℤ

Eros, Imagination, and Sentimentality

INCORPORATING SEXUALITY INTO PRACTICE

BROTHER DAVID: There's a lot of confusion about sexuality in the Church and among religious people generally, I think. I hope we can look at this as a question of practice—how does one channel sexual power so as to be conducive to practice?—but eventually it boils down to a personal question, so I'll begin from my personal perspective as a celibate.

One of my greatest complaints against the present state of religious life in my own tradition is that, in religious formation, there's been little instruction for dealing with one's sexuality as a celibate. No dos, only don'ts. This isn't a recent problem. Historically, Christian monastic tradition has taught very little about sexuality. In the hundreds of sayings of the Desert Fathers, for instance, the number explicitly addressing the matter of sex is very low. Sexuality is ignored, more or less, and when it's not ignored, it's treated with a negative slant. In the last two hundred years or so, I suppose it was practically universal that, as an older monk once said to me, "When we entered the monastery, we were simply told to leave sex behind." That was all. That was the end of it. Sex was to have no place in one's life from that moment on.

Fortunately, in the last two decades or so, there's been a great rediscovery of the body, of embodiment, within the monastic tradition. I'm 100 percent in favor of all that. Certainly, living as a celibate doesn't mean that one cuts oneself off from sexuality or freezes it or leaves it behind. When I was a child, we had the riddle "Which dog barks with its tail?" The answer was "All dogs!" because no dog takes off its tail in order to bark. Similarly, none of us take off our sexuality in order to chant in the choir or to meditate. Whatever we do, we always do it as whole men or whole women.

I understand sexuality as one manifestation of the life power, of the power that's there, and I feel that it enters into everything we do, particularly into every relationship between humans. It's the bodily expression of our relatedness to others. This doesn't mean, in most interactions, that we have an explicit awareness of anything sexual involved. It's simply there, just as a dog's tail is there while it's barking, but the dog isn't particularly aware that it's there. Sexuality also expresses relatedness to ourselves, which is extremely important to me but largely overlooked in society.

Therefore, a great challenge before the Christian monastic community now is to learn how to deal with sexuality in a celibate way. The majority of teachers whom I know and respect would agree with the statement that it's irresponsible to accept new monks in our climate and society and supposedly prepare them for a celibate life without giving them any instruction about how to use their sexuality for spiritual improvement.

AITKEN RŌSHI: Or even to acknowledge their sexuality.

BD: That's the first step, of course, and I think it's been taken universally by now. But it's only the most forward-looking teachers who are saying that we have to go to the next step of developing some sort of method to actually teach people how to use their sex in a way that's compatible with a celibate life or, I would say, that makes a celibate life possible.

Now, through the encounter with Eastern traditions, we're on the verge of profiting from a centuries-old, and maybe millennia-old, tradition of dealing directly and positively with sexual energy in a religious context. Some people are beginning to make use of this Eastern heritage, particularly of Tantra.[1] In a recent conversation with Bede Griffiths, a very important person in the dialogue between East and West, I asked how he dealt with sexuality among his novices, and he said, "Well, of course, we give instruction in channeling the kundalini. Of course we do that methodically."[2] There was no opportunity to go into any detail, but he said that the Eastern teachers who come now to the West work mostly with raising your kundalini, which he felt wasn't particularly helpful to Westerners as a starting point. He said, "I believe you first have to help Westerners go down and then bring the energy up."

AR: With fewer specifics, I think that's the Zen way, too: to settle into and gather that energy so that it's focused and concentrated and cannot be random.

BD: I'm pretty sure that's what he meant.

AR: I've always felt very uneasy about the notion of raising one's kundalini. I've felt that, without someone present who's highly skilled, that's the way to madness.

---

[1] *Tantra:* Sanskrit for text, here referring to the highly developed sexual symbolism and methods of practice developed in the Vajrayāna school of Buddhism.

[2] Bede Griffiths, since deceased, was a British-born Catholic monastic who lived thirty-eight years in India and found in its religious traditions, as he put it, "the other half of my soul." Kundalini: a Sanskrit term denoting an energy normally residing at the base of the spine. Kundalini yoga entails learning to master this energy and use it for spiritual ends.

BD: But with someone highly skilled present, it could be a most valuable exercise.

AR: Liberating. Some people are particularly oriented toward kundalini. I've had a few students like this who somehow found their spiritual home in the Zen milieu, but it's not within my area of expertise.

BD: How would you, in very general terms, advise someone who asks, "How shall I deal with my sexual power?"

AR: Certainly, it's important to have a channel for sexual power. That might mean having a partner, but it might also mean finding a fulfilling means of sublimating it. Sublimation has developed a rather negative connotation in our society, unjustly so, as though it were a kind of denial. Certainly, there are very happy people, outside the monastery as well as in, who've chosen celibacy. In fact, there's a kind of movement in modern culture, a movement of singles who deliberately choose to be celibate.

BD: We meet them all the time. Some come to become monks, but others come just to spend time in the monastery. They're often very inspiring people.

AR: Their energies are freed up. I think this is something that older people come to naturally in the course of marriage, too: in time, their love is freed up, so to speak.

BD: Sublimation literally means "to lift over the lintel," to lift something to the next level—and perhaps to the next level, then the one after that. It can be seen as an aspect of refining one's life, as we discussed earlier. The real challenge of the spiritual path is to refine our lives in every way.

There's one other aspect to celibate sexuality I haven't mentioned yet, which is that the raising and sublimation of crude sexuality (crude not in a negative sense but just like crude oil: unrefined) is far easier in a warm, affectionate community than in a cold community. In fact, it's almost impossible in a cold community because the natural longing of the human heart for warmth and intimacy will get mixed up with a need for physical intimacy, and this is totally confusing, particularly to younger members. When there's real warmth and kinship among members of a community, a monastic community or otherwise, sublimation of sexuality is far easier to achieve. We who belong to monastic communities must be aware of our responsibility to offer one another real warmth, which is totally different from the back-slapping chumminess one sometimes finds.

Let's examine another part of this question: what are the symptoms when sex is getting in the way of your practice?

AR: Your thoughts tell you. Your spontaneous fantasies, your dreams, and little turns of conduct all tell you—and not just during meditation. In a psychologist's office, I once saw a cartoon that had two panels. In both of them, a psychologist was reading instructions for a test, but in the first one the student was male and in the second the student was female. The psychologist was depicted reading the instructions to the man with a straight face and to the woman with a broad smile. This cartoon was posted in the psychologist's office as a reminder of this little turn of conduct, one of many that can color an entire situation. To be self-aware, we need to learn to pick up these clues, and we can learn by watching others and reflecting on how we behave: do I treat my male and female students differently?

BD: When you speak about dreams and fantasies and so forth, if I understand you correctly, you're saying it's a sign that sexuality is getting in the way of our practice if we're preoccupied, not just if we have sexual dreams. It's a persistent pattern, a preoccupation, that we should be alert for.

AR: Exactly. What rises to your mind when you sit down to meditate? If it's the practice and there are just incidental distractions as you go along in the course of the sitting, and you gradually get to the place where dream images come and go rather than plans and schemes and memories, then you're doing well. But if you're carried away by some sexual drama, you know that you've fallen into a trap.

BD: And if we expand what you just now said to the wider kind of practice we're concerned with, we could say it's no problem if sexual attraction, sexual imagery, and so forth enter into consciousness here and there, but if a person begins to think of others consistently in sexual terms, then there's something a little askew.

To broaden the point a little bit, what about sensuality? Would you say that sensuality is always bad for practice? Or maybe I should say *sensuousness,* since *sensuality* tends to have a negative connotation. Is sensuousness bad for practice?

AR: No, of course not. Sensuality certainly suffuses the human psyche, just as sexuality does. If we weren't sensual, we'd have no capacity for love, as I understand that word *sensual.*

BD: I think that's a legitimate understanding of the word, but it largely has at least a slightly pejorative connotation, implying overindulgence in sensual pleasure.

AR: Overindulgence in sensual pleasure, like any other overindulgence, can get in the way of practice, of course.

BD: What I call sensuality implies overindulgence. We agree that it's incompatible with healthy practice. But can that energy be transformed into something positive for practice?

AR: I think any human quality can be transformed into an asset for practice.

BD: And I feel the more energy there is, the better. In choosing candidates for the monkhood, I get the impression some monastics regard the dullest candidates as the most promising because they make no mistakes. But they also don't do anything very positive. I'd much rather accept somebody who makes lots of mistakes but has a lot of energy that could be channeled in the right direction.

AR: And what is sensuality but energy?

THE PLACE OF FANTASY AND IMAGINATION

BD: We've mentioned that fantasy, specifically sexual fantasy, is a normal aspect of the psyche, but teachers of spirituality don't seem to give due credit to fantasy and imagination, right?

AR: Right.

BD: You do though.

AR: I do, and I know others who do. Certainly Sōen Rōshi was outstanding in this respect. Unfortunately, some Zen teachers of our time actively discourage students even from reading!

BD: What would you say to them?

AR: When I meet refugees, so to speak, from those teachers, I urge them to catch up with their reading, take up their musical instruments again, and so forth. I work with these students, encouraging them as best they can to fulfill themselves in their particular talents or interests. We're all of a piece! If one side of a person is stultified, the whole person is stultified.

BD: It's my assumption that the goal of practice is to come fully alive, in the sense intended in the tenth chapter of the Gospel of John, where Jesus says, "I've come that they may have life and have life in fullness." [Jn. 10:10] If one accepts this, then all areas of life have to be cultivated. For a time, however, under certain conditions, it might be necessary to forgo playing your instrument or even forgo reading certain things that you'd normally read.

AR: Of course you can't play a trumpet in your monastery, I imagine.

BD: Right. Certain limitations are placed on life in the interest of reaching a higher goal. But basically I think we should cultivate all our various talents.

AR: Recall the case of Hopkins again: he was a student of poetry at Oxford and a friend of Bridges and other poets and writers. Then he became a Catholic, joined the Jesuit order, and decided on his own to forgo poetry. In seven years, he wrote only two poems, poems that were very slight and composed for particular occasions. Then came the news of the wreck of the *Deutschland*. On board were seven nuns escaping from repression in Germany. Hopkins was profoundly saddened by this news, as was his entire community. His prior said, "I wish someone would write a poem about this," and suddenly Hopkins felt released, freed to write. The resulting poem, "The Wreck of the *Deutschland*," isn't his best poem, but from that time on, for the rest of his short life, he wrote most effusively and beautifully.

BD: It may not be his best poem, but it's a wonderful poem, I think. There are many important things in it, including the phrase "ground of being" that Paul Tillich later introduced into theological language as an alternative to the theistic term *God*. That phrase comes from "The Wreck of the *Deutschland*," and Hopkins also refers to God there as the "granite shore."

AR: It seems that Hopkins was unconsciously building his talent during those seven years and that, in a sense, they were very productive years.

BD: So as a Zen teacher you encourage at the same time the complete cleansing of the mind of imagination while doing zazen and, at other times, full use of the powers of imagination.

AR: It isn't really possible to cleanse the mind, as you put it, if there's lots of pent-up, unfulfilled stuff in your head and your heart. It'll always be pushing forth in your zazen. So when a musician, for example, comes to live and practice at our zendo for a while, I encourage him or her to go to the music school at the University of Hawaii and arrange to use one of the practice rooms. Some of them leap at the chance, but others, I think, feel a bit like Hopkins and opt to put music aside for a while.

BD: Right in line with this matter is the question of beauty. How important is beauty to the life of practice? We've already touched on this in discussing asceticism, and when you put flowers into the vases here, you anticipated and answered it again in the most vivid way. Do you want to say anything further?

AR: I remember Sōen Rōshi taking me to the room in the monastery that I was to occupy for the next few months. When we arrived, he gestured about the room and said, in his limited English, "You may decorate!" I think it's very important to have reminders in our homes of the beauties of the world and the created beauties of our fellow beings.

BD: One kind of beauty it seems particularly important to cultivate today is that of simplicity—stripping things down to beauty rather than dressing them up, adding more. There's too much decoration going on. I've sometimes challenged people in institutions by saying, "What could you take out of this room to make it more beautiful?" rather than "What could you put into it?" On the surface, that would be the opposite of Sōen Rōshi, but it's the same intention, exactly the same intention. To a large extent we've lost our sense of the beauty of the thing itself, undecorated, without anything added. Bare wood, for example. The Japanese have cultivated this aesthetic, and so have the Scandinavians: unpainted wood. Just letting things be themselves.

AR: There's also a beauty of revealing what lies hidden in things, as John Donne says in his poem "The Crosse." The key lines are "Carvers do not faces make, / But that away, which hid them there, do take."

BD: It reminds me of a little boy watching a woodcarver chipping away on a block of wood and saying with the greatest admiration, "How did you know that horse was in there?" The Eskimos also think of their carvers as the liberators of what they carve—not as making something but as liberating it, allowing a seal or a whale or whatever to emerge from the stone. This is closely related to spiritual growth. If a person thinks of beauty in that way, it eases the release of his or her own true self. It's all of one piece.

AR: Yes, and it does entail stripping away the unnecessary decorations.

THE PROBLEM OF SENTIMENTALITY

BD: How do you define sentimentality, and how do you avoid it? I look forward to what you have to say about this not only as a teacher of Zen but also as a poet.

AR: The first thing I think of is a conversation I once had with W. S. Merwin about use of the word *blossoms*.[3] The conventional translation of the Japanese word *hana* is *blossoms,* but he told me, "Never say *blossoms.* Always say *flowers.*" This pointer shouldn't be taken absolutely but has been very helpful to me as an example. When you consider the phrases "cherry blossoms" and "cherry flowers," you see they create very different impressions.

The sentimental is the word of the word. It's a pandering to those who don't want to get at the word but want to be content with the word of the word. The word *blossoms* may once have been straightforward and true, but it's become what you might call false poetry, poetry that's lifeless.

---

[3] Merwin, one of America's foremost living poets and author of many fine translations, studied with Aitken Rōshi for several years.

BD: Something thought rather than felt. It's like a little essay that rhymes.

AR: Yes, a little essay contrived to create a certain sentiment, a certain feeling. In "Trees"—"I think that I shall never see / A poem lovely as a tree"—Joyce Kilmer is just rehashing a lot of things that have been said before in a most profound way. He's taking bits and pieces of those profound expressions and making a kind of collage out of them, not speaking from experience.

BD: That's the main point, as I see it: in sentimentality, we're trying to whip up sentiments, but the words aren't connected with our deepest experience. In genuine expression, deep experience flows into the moment.

AR: It's not that all popular art is sentimental. Genuine expression can be found in popular art and popular music, while gallery art and orchestral music can certainly be sentimental.

BD: Yes. Conformity to some external standards or expectations rather than to your authentic self—that's sentimentality.

AR: Yet conformity, in the sense of learning from others, may play an important part in genuine creativity. Again, that remark of Hopkins is pertinent: "The effect of studying masterpieces is to make me admire and do otherwise." We need others' inspiration. Studying the history of late nineteenth century Western art, we learn clearly that the Impressionists influenced each other, but looking at their work, we see they're distinctly different—all the great ones, at least. Derivative, sentimental painters adopted the Impressionist manner later on, but there's really no conformity among the great Impressionists. Rather, it was an instance of mutual inspiration. It would really have been impossible for one of those Impressionists to appear all by himself.

BD: That's right. And the phrase, "Admire the masters and do otherwise" applies equally to spiritual practice, doesn't it?

AR: Exactly. When we look at people in the same lineage of Zen teachers, we find very, very different personalities and very different life-styles and life work.

BD: Another way to detect sentimentality and distinguish it from genuine feeling suddenly occurred to me. In genuine feeling, the deeper it is, the more ambiguous it is. In genuine art, the deeper it is, the deeper the ambiguities. I think it was Leonard Bernstein who said that something he admired about jazz is that, even when it's at its most exuberant, it has a note of sadness. When it's at its most forlorn, it has a note of hope in it. That's the kind of ambiguity I mean. Sentimental music is either all happiness or all lugubrious; it lacks this ambiguity.

Maybe if we check our own feelings for this ambiguity, it would serve as an indication of the extent to which we're really connected with our deepest sources. I'm concerned about sentimentality because in practice, maybe less so in Zen than in the Christian context, sentimentality is something that quite frequently crops up.

AR: Maybe the sentimental person is taking himself or herself too seriously.

BD: And therefore misses the ambiguity.

AR: Or misses the possibility of real creativity, which lies in the unexpected. One of the joys of Mozart, for example, is that when you expect him to go up a third, he goes up an octave and a third or down an octave and a third, or maybe not even a third but a seventh instead.

BD: And that, in turn, makes the music true to life—because life *is* surprise.

☙ II ☙

Bitter Emotions

THE FIRES OF WRATH

BROTHER DAVID: Is there a constructive way of dealing with deep-seated anger?

AITKEN RŌSHI: Yes, of course, though it's by no means easy. Among the Ten Grave Precepts of Mahayana Buddhism, the only one that explicitly deals with an emotion is the one on anger. Even sex isn't dealt with in emotional terms; it's dealt with in terms of conduct. In translating the precept on anger, I've modified it a little by rendering it as "not indulging in anger." I'm convinced that anger itself is a virtue and that the problem lies in *indulging* our anger.

BD: I'm so glad you say that!

AR: In its pure form, anger is a teaching. In the New Testament, there are at least two instances of Jesus losing his temper, both very instructive. When he cleansed the temple of money changers, for example, you can be sure that his anger was quite hot, probably white-hot. Pure anger.

I often think of my old teacher Yasutani Rōshi in connection with anger. He was one of too many children in a terribly poor family, so his mother took him to a temple for the priests to raise, which was then a custom in Japan. He was five years old at the time this happened, and you can imagine its impact on him. He grew up to be a very angry boy and a very angry man, contentious until the day he died. But in his mature years, when I knew him, his anger had become pure. He wasn't the least bit sensitive about personal criticism; he wouldn't get angry if you told him that his collar was dirty, for example. If you misspoke about the Dharma, however, he'd get exercised, and if you misspoke in a serious way, he'd take you to task in a most fiery and vivid fashion. In my book *A Zen Wave,* there's a photograph of him lecturing, in which you can see the heat of his passion.[1]

In *Zen in English Literature,* R. H. Blyth tells a marvelous story from the life of Robert Louis Stevenson.[2] It seems that one day Stevenson came upon a man beating his dog and intervened to make him stop. "It's not your dog," the man replied and would have continued, but Stevenson said, "It's *God's* dog, and I'm here to protect it!" That kind of cosmic anger changes the world. Gandhi was an angry man. King was an angry man.

BD: Many reformers are angry people in this sense. I must ask you to backtrack for a moment, though, and to say something about how we can get from the point where Yasutani Rōshi was angry because he felt he'd been personally betrayed to the anger of his later years, which was directed toward injustice and ignorance. I follow the distinction you're making between anger that's impure and anger that's pure, but in the process of purification, what is sifted out?

AR: Let me quote the *Ts'ai-ken t'an:* "When the wind blows through the bamboo grove, the trunks clatter against one an-

---

[1] *A Zen Wave: Bashō's Haiku and Zen* (New York: Weatherhill, 1978).
[2] Blyth was Aitken Rōshi's mentor and this book his gateway to Zen. See the Introduction.

other. When it has passed, the grove is quiet once more."[3] If your consciousness is essentially quiet, then anger will come up appropriately and die down appropriately. It seems to me that a parent who says to a child, "Get off of there! I don't want you standing on the table!" is giving a pointed instruction to the child, and the child will think, "Wow! I won't do *that* again," and then it passes. It's gone. It's like an incision that heals immediately.

BD: I understand what you're saying now. As you know, I had the great privilege also of having Yasutani Rōshi as a teacher, and I think I understand his ability not to take it at all personally if someone commented on his dirty collar or on another small imperfection. As a perfectionist, which he definitely was, he heard so many voices criticizing him continuously from within that the little voice on the outside that also criticized him was insignificant; he was so used to criticism that it didn't faze him at all anymore.

AR: I don't think Yasutani Rōshi was hearing those voices all the time. I think his mind was quiet by that time in his life.

BD: It's really not so important whether it applies to Yasutani Rōshi or not, but would it make sense that the process of dealing with our anger has something to do with transcending those inner voices to reach the quiet you speak of?

AR: The transcending process is a matter of finding that place in your heart of hearts where nothing moves, where all is at rest.

BD: In Saint Paul's letters, there's a passage relevant to this discussion: "Go ahead and be angry, but do not sin. Let the sun

---

[3] The *Ts'ai-ken t'an* is a collection of aphorisms, brief homilies, and fables by the sixteenth-century Chinese writer Hung Ying-ming. For English translations, see Yaichiro Isobe, *Musings of a Chinese Vegetarian* (Tokyo: Yuhodo, 1926), p. 69, and William Scott Wilson, *Roots of Wisdom: Saikontan* (New York: Kodansha, 1985), p. 51.

not set over your anger." [Eph. 4:26] Sin means alienation, so he's saying, go ahead and be angry, but don't let it alienate you from others. Be angry from a place that isn't alienated. Also, the warning not to let the sun set over your anger may either mean to make up before evening or, on a deeper level, to let your anger be transparent to that light of the sun. Let it not be a dark anger; let it be a light anger.

Thomas Aquinas says that anger is the extra energy needed to overcome obstacles. It's like that extra bit of gas you get when you step on the gas pedal hard when you go uphill. That's the best of the Christian tradition on this question, and it fully agrees with what you say about anger as a positive thing, something desirable to have.

AR: It sounds to me as if Saint Paul was drawing the line between being angry and indulging in anger. This leads to another question: do you distinguish between anger and hatred?

BD: It's difficult to speak about this in English because the word *anger* almost inevitably has overtones of hatred. A positive anger would have to be an anger completely free of hatred.

AR: Do you think hatred can ever be a virtue?

BD: This is even more subtle. My answer is yes, if it's a hatred that isn't malevolent.

AR: To hate fascism, for example.

BD: It's a hatred in the sense of a complete opposition, the hatred that's implied in the injunction to love our enemies. To fulfill it, we need to have enemies. But to have enemies means to be opposed to others in a hatred that isn't alienated, isn't spiteful, isn't hateful, in the usual sense. A hatred that's a loving hatred. The English language doesn't allow us to say that very easily.

AR: Does the German language?

BD: No, I don't know of a language that allows this. Maybe we'll have to develop it or invent it. But I think we see eye-to-eye on this.

One more thing comes to mind in connection with this question. Do you think dealing with deep-seated anger constructively means to make it *more* deep-seated? At the deepest level, our anger is pure energy that can be used for good. But on a superficial level, anger becomes self-centered in a negative sense, thus impure.

AR: Deep-seated anger in this sense is one that rises from a perception that some situation or activity isn't in keeping with my purest vision, my vision of things as they are in their ultimate nature.

BD: Springing from that deepest center, your anger is an expression of desire to restore the world. It's an expression of practice because it springs from a point where I and whatever or whoever I'm angry with are one.

AR: *I'm* not doing it right, in other words. It's not that you "out there" are wrong.

BD: That's right. Dealing constructively with anger may mean going down to the source of the purest anger and letting that gush forth to purify the more superficial sort of anger. Something like that. Very difficult in practice.

AR: Indeed. There's almost always a tinge of self-justification in my instructive anger. Sometimes more than a tinge.

BD: When monks spoke about purifying our motives, Father Damasus used to say something that's been very helpful to me. Jokingly but with a great deal of seriousness, he'd say, "Don't worry about purifying your motives. Simply know that they aren't pure, and proceed."

SHAME

BD: How do you deal with what T. S. Eliot called "the shame of motives late revealed"?

AR: A confession is good for the soul, for starters. Then, if one's motives are truly revealed, accurately revealed, there's only one recourse and that's to acknowledge this failing to the other party. If one's motives are only part bad, as is often the case, acknowledge that part and don't be in haste to add the more favorable motives. Wait and see if those motives aren't suggested by the other party in the course of the conversation.

BD: The quotation comes from a passage in the fourth of the *Four Quartets,* where Eliot speaks of the gifts reserved for age, and I think it probably *is* a question that's of greatest interest to older people. He lists these gifts, which many people wouldn't think of as gifts at all, in the context of looking back over one's life:

> . . . the rending pain of re-enactment
> Of all that you have done, and been; the shame
> Of motives late revealed, and the awareness
> Of things ill done and done to others' harm,
> Which once you took for exercise of virtue.

You intended well, but in retrospect, you see that what you did was done to others' harm. A few lines later, he says,

> From wrong to wrong the exasperated spirit
> Proceeds, unless restored by that refining fire
> Where you must move in measure, like a dancer.

I was struck by this idea of the refining fire and motives late revealed, the refining fire that refines the motives. Then, in the following section appear these lines, which are really a quotation from Julian or Norwich, the great English mystic:

> And all shall be well and
> All manner of thing shall be well

By the purification of the motive
In the ground of our beseeching.

That's the great task. The ground of our beseeching would be the same ground, the heart of hearts, to which we come back again and again.

AR: A little different, isn't it? The place of great peace and unity is the dōjō, which is the Japanese translation of Bodhimanda, the seat under the Bodhi Tree where the Buddha had his great enlightenment. It seems to me the ground of our beseeching is a tao, a path, not a place so much as an act.

BD: I think that one could make a good case that Buddha sitting under the Bodhi Tree is the act of beseeching. *Beseeching* is a good word for what's going on in that place: it's the utmost effort, the ultimate existential effort, of the whole person. So the two coincide, more or less. One is the static aspect, the other the dynamic aspect.

AR: I agree.

BD: I think what happens to the Buddha under the Bodhi Tree is the purification of the motives of the ground of his beseeching. It's enfolded in the mythology of the different temptations he undergoes there. That's purification of the motives, isn't it?

AR: He was no longer obstructed by delusions of self, no longer handicapped by preoccupations and self-deceptions, so he could see that all beings are the Buddha.

BD: But the way this is presented in the mythology, with Māra and his forces coming to tempt and divert the Buddha from his quest—this could be understood as the very process of practice. It's not meant to show that he'd overcome this already and was impervious to temptation but rather that the tempters are himself, in a sense.

AR: In a very real sense.

BD: The temptation itself is the process of the purification. Applying this to "the shame of motives late revealed," how do we deal with that shame? By purification of the motive in the ground of our beseeching.

AR: I'd say that it's by the practice of mustering body and mind to a single point. Of course this is what zazen is about, but it's not limited just to zazen. Simone Weil has a wonderful passage about summoning up all one's attention and focusing it on a matter that's not clear, putting everything else to one side. She had a breakthrough experience working with George Herbert's poem "Love," which is quite plainspoken but was a very elusive poem for her because she was reading it in her second language. It was also difficult because it's a profoundly Christian poem, and she herself wasn't Christian to begin with. So she had to devote herself to it fully and completely, and by doing so she got to the point that was at the very heart of her existential doubts. That's the way of practice.

BD: That's the way to purify the motive, ultimately.

AR: Yes, I think that all things follow if you allow them to. By "purifying one's motive" in zazen, I mean dropping everything else. "Purifying one's motive" in the larger dimension of practice is surely devoting yourself to the task at hand and letting everything else go. If your task, so to speak, is a conversation, then you're devoting yourself to the other person and to absorbing the explicit and implicit meanings that are coming forth.

BD: Yes, this single-minded attention Simone Weil reached— that would always be there. The image that comes to mind is of a magnifying glass that collects the rays of the sun, focusing them to a single point such that they can burn a hole in a piece of paper. This burning purification, that refining fire, is the image that fits with what you said.

AR: I think so, and it raises a related point that's very important: this process can be used for any purpose. Just as an unhappy little boy can use a magnifying glass to burn insects, an exploit-ive businessman can use meditation to serve his own greedy ends. So although we're purifying our motives along the way, a pure motive must be present in practice from the beginning.

BD: As I'm getting older, I deal quite frequently with "motives late revealed" and "things done to others' harm that once you took for exercise of virtue." A big trap is to feel there's nothing we can do about these errors anymore. "That's something in the past," we say to ourselves. "It's over. How can you remedy it in the present if it's already happened?" For me, the purification process works this way: I recognize that the error was necessary, in some sense. It was necessary schooling for me. It's not in itself good or desirable, but unless I had made this mistake, I wouldn't now be where I am. Now *use* this insight in a single-minded way to purify the motive.

AR: I'd carry it a step further. Even if the person you wronged is dead and gone, it's possible to hold a kind of conversation with him or her. Of course, if the person is still alive, it's possible to write a letter or place a phone call and make this purification more than just an individual matter.

BD: I'm glad you said that. I think that's absolutely necessary.

JEALOUSY AND REJECTION

BD: Another of the bitter and difficult emotions is jealousy. When one really loves someone, how can one avoid jealousy?

AR: First of all, I'm not so sure jealousy should always be avoided. When they marry, a couple creates a new being—the marriage. From this new being may come children and family. It's the responsibility of each spouse to contribute to the good health of the marriage, to nurture and protect this being.

BD: You're using the word *being* in a very interesting and un-usual way here. . . .

AR: A being is anything that exists. Even imaginary entities are beings, in this broadest sense: a gargoyle is a being, a unicorn is a being.

BD: In other words, it needn't exist in reality. It can be a being of imagination.

AR: But a being of imagination is real! It has a birth and a life and a death, like any other being.

BD: In the imagination.

AR: Yes—and the imagination is part of the universe.

BD: Sure. I'm not denying it. The imagination not only is part of the universe, it can have an enormous influence on events. Just think of the influence that unicorns have had on people.

AR: To go back to the being of marriage, if the conduct of one spouse seems to threaten the life of that being, then the anxiety of the other to protect the marriage is aroused. If we call this jealousy, then I think it's a positive kind of response. How one *handles* it is another matter.

Of course, the negative form of jealousy is the one we're more familiar with: the perceived offense to me if my wife is overtly or covertly flirting with somebody else. I think this may be related to anxiety to protect the relationship, but it's been blown out of proportion. Some people respond with protectiveness to every little conversation their spouses have with others.

BD: The negative kind of jealousy is characterized, I'd say, by possessiveness. That's obviously destructive, whereas the kind of jealousy that you've described is constructive, one that builds up the being, as you call it, of the marriage. I see much the same thing in the context of friendship: a friendship may be protected in order to let it overflow and enrich all others, while a friendship that's cliquish or ingrown—jealous in the negative sense—is destructive not only for the community within which it's set but also for the two friends themselves.

AR: This sense of a marriage as a being is quite real and power-ful, I think, though usually unconscious. We celebrate the birth of that being at the wedding ceremony, take delight in nurtur-ing it through its growth and the appearance of children, and mourn its death if a divorce occurs. I'm sure you've experienced such mourning on many occasions.

BD: As divorces become more frequent, it's becoming more and more necessary to ritualize divorce. I don't know whether you do this at your zendo, but a positive closure with the ritual, just as you have a ritual for marriage, can be an enormous help in this mourning process.

AR: We don't have such a ceremony. I've encouraged closure through mediation and through direct conversations, but I like the idea of a ritual.

BD: How are we to handle rejection by those we love?

AR: This is a source of deep-seated pain because it's a rejection of an affinity that arises from mysterious sources. When we cul-tivate an affinity with someone, either through imagination or with the other's active participation, and then we're rejected, it's a kind of death, and we mourn it as we would a death.

BD: People sometimes actually die from being rejected.

AR: Yes, we know, at least statistically, that cancer often follows a betrayal, rejection, disappointment.

BD: A rejection is deeply wounding because we turn our most vulnerable side to those we most love. Also, it's a deep shattering of our self-respect because our self-respect tends to be built par-ticularly on the opinions of those whom we respect and treasure.

I wonder how often it happens that two friends or lovers really love one another with what one could call equal affection. Of course, there's really no way to measure or compare levels of affection, but in general terms, at least you could say that equal affection occurs if the two people are totally investing their love in each other. How often does that happen in your opinion? Often, rarely, hardly ever?

A R : I don't know, but I remember a *senryū* that suggests a way of making the measurement. Do you know the senryū, a Japanese form of satirical verse?

B D : Like a haiku but about people.

A R : In this case, about a couple walking together under a single umbrella.

> The umbrella tips away
> from the one who
> loves the most.

In other words, whoever feels the greater love will tip the umbrella to protect the other one.

B D : That's lovely. I'll have to watch how many couples carry their umbrellas straight up! The pair that loves one another equally is a big theme in literature, but from what my friends confide to me, it seems relatively rare. If there are four people, instead of A loving B and B loving A, while C and D also love each other mutually, what often happens is that A loves B, B loves C, C loves D, and D loves A—it goes around in a circle. There's a big mess, and I keep asking myself, "Why is this so? Is there a deeper meaning to it?" The only thing I've come up with is that maybe we'd get stuck if couples were paired off perfectly; the love would get ingrown, and we'd lose our sense of multicentered being. Maybe this somehow is intended to broaden our love and not get it fixed on only one person.

A R : It seems to me that in cases like A loves B, B loves C, and so on, there's not a clear vision of what marriage is. It's important not only to love the other but also to devote oneself to what we're building together. When one's focus is on that, then the occasional experience of falling in love outside the marriage will be no more than a momentary bad cold, so to speak.

BD: Yes, but I'd give a very positive meaning to that experience, also. I've often told married people, "For heaven's sakes, be *grateful* when you fall in love. The more often, the better! Just be aware of what you do with that energy. Channel it into your married life if at all possible, in exactly the same way celibates have to channel it into their celibate life." Falling in love ignites an enormous amount of energy, and I think it's a tremendous gift that nature makes us fall in love every so often, if we can only learn to channel that energy positively. It would be absolutely wasteful not to make use of that energy in our spiritual life.

As I've said, in a healthy marriage this energy can be channeled back into the marriage itself. Ideally, the other spouse even will be able to extend his or her love to the third person involved, and in this way, the love within a marriage or a friendship can overflow. Another way in which this energy could be channeled is into caring, into being gentler with everybody. I think this whole method of channeling feelings of love may be more obvious to celibates than to married people because it's such a necessary part of our practice, but everyone can learn it and practice it.

ℵ 12 ℤ

Dealing with Others

BROTHER DAVID: How can we liberate ourselves from being ruled by others' expectations?

AITKEN RŌSHI: It seems to me that, fundamentally, this liberation is a matter of what I might call spiritual confidence. In the mythology of Buddhism, we read that just after the Buddha was born, he took seven steps in each of the cardinal directions, pointed to the heavens with one hand and to the earth with the other, and declared, "Above the heavens, below the heavens, only I, alone and sacred." (An alternative translation is "only I, the World-Honored One.") It seems like a very conceited thing for a little kid to say, but that's taking it too literally. The point is that *this* [indicating his own body] is the unique body of the Buddha.

In my early days of Zen training in Japan, I used to be puzzled by the fact that the monks seemed to equate confidence with realization. I thought to myself, "Isn't confidence a matter of the ego?" I was very confused about ego and all of those

133

things at the time. The understanding that you yourself are the Buddha is a very humbling experience, but at the same time, it gives us the confidence to stand on our own two feet. It gives us the confidence to be open to, but not ruled by, others' expectations—to be open to the advice and suggestions of others but to make our own decisions.

BD: How do we get to that point?

AR: With this realization of the unique Buddha (or, in your terms, the experience that God is me) comes the potential to do something unique, something personally creative. Children are always looking for this in themselves: "What can I do that will be especially me?" We continue that search throughout our lives—a cultivation of the "especially me." What is it? As we go along, we reach milestones of confirmation, points where we see "*This* is what I am!" This is a revelation of character, not at all contradicting the fact that all perceptions are essentially empty, that there's nothing fixed or specific we can identify as the self or its potential.

As we go along, reaching these little milestones, we gradually develop our confidence. The problem in our society is that it's set up so that people with some particular kinds of potential, such as making money or influencing others, have the best chance to fulfill themselves. The masses of people work in very unsatisfactory, unfulfilling kinds of jobs and have relatively little chance to reach these milestones.

BD: It must be possible, however, for a person who works at an unfulfilling job and has to continue that job, living in a society very limited in what it acknowledges as valid self-expression—it must be possible within that job and within this society, for a person who really suffers from being ruled by others' expectations to liberate himself or herself gradually, step-by-step.

AR: I think so.

BD: If I understand you correctly when you speak of little milestones, it would work something like this: that person would start in the smallest way, saying, perhaps, "All right, this evening, what will I do that's really myself and gives me satisfaction?" Then she or he does something that's a little out of the ordinary, just simply does it and sees it work, sees that it was something unexpected and takes pride and satisfaction in it.

AR: Yes, and it's very important to put oneself in a place where such experiences are possible. For example, if one is oriented toward ideas, it's important to browse in a library or in a bookstore, taking down books and looking at them and putting them back until you find one that really speaks to you at this particular time, then to buy or borrow it and read it and talk about it.

BD: That's a good example. I'd agree that it's important to have this environment, but it's also important to stress that someone caught in the trap of being ruled by others' expectations shouldn't wait until the right environment comes around. Look at this very environment in which you find yourself, and see if there's already a little loophole where you can do what isn't expected. I'm thinking of really little things—a woman putting a flower in her hair one morning before she goes to the office, for instance, or a man paying a compliment to somebody under circumstances where no compliment is expected. Just tiny little things like that.

As you rightly indicated in referring to the baby Buddha who points to the sky and the earth, an act like this is anchored in our deepest reality. It isn't just some little attempt to be pleasant and make friends. From the perspective of the Christian tradition, it's anchored in "To all those who received Him, He gave power to be sons and daughters of God," which is in the prologue to the Gospel according to John [Jn. 1:12]. Or again in John, Jesus prays that every human being may be one with divine reality—"as you, Father, and I are one." [Jn. 17:21] If we're anchored at this deepest level of experience, we can be creative and free in the smallest detail of daily practice, in wearing a flower behind the ear, in borrowing the books we really like, in doing something else that isn't expected, even in saying a creative no to something that *is* expected.

PRACTICING FRIENDLINESS

BD: If warmth and intimacy don't come naturally to us, how can we best cultivate them?

AR: I got a lesson on this one from an episode in the comic strip "Beetle Bailey," which is set in an army camp. In this episode, the super-shy young officer, Lieutenant Fuzz, is asking others how to make conversation at an upcoming party. They advise him to write down some lines, memorize them, and come forth with them at the right moment. The final box of the comic strip shows him at the party, nervously looking at his notes and saying, "Hello."

That's an important lesson. If warmth and intimacy don't come naturally, how do you best cultivate them? With practice. If you meet someone you know and you're not sure whether to hug or just shake hands, then you hug. You practice being intimate.

BD: In other words, it's a little like physical therapy. An injured arm or leg may be too stiff to move all the way, but even the stiffest limb will have a small margin of mobility. So you move it in that little margin and every day, imperceptibly, gain a bit more flexibility. But you do have to work at it.

AR: Right! You have to take yourself in hand and do it. You can't say to yourself, "I'm shy. I'm a wallflower." You have to get out there and practice—and it has to be real practice, practice from the heart, not the superficial, Dale Carnegie kind of practice that creates just a hollow pseudocordiality. The practice we're talking about can be likened to the practice necessary to become a musician: you sit down at the piano and practice Mozart.

BD: But first you have to practice a lot of scales.

AR: You have to practice a lot of scales, then you have to practice a lot of pieces Mozart wrote when he was five years old, and gradually, gradually, you can become more intimate with Mozart. When I've counseled people in this way, some have responded, "But it isn't *honest* for me to express feelings that I don't have." It is, too! You may be too stiff to feel such things at the moment, but all of us want warmth and intimacy, and we can honestly practice friendliness on that basis.

BD: This is a question of layers of honesty. Can I honestly act otherwise than I feel? Is that honesty? If I feel, for instance, really peeved with someone, is it honest to behave in a civil and friendly way? My answer is yes: it's more honest to behave in a friendly manner than to act out feelings of rejection and so forth, because friendliness springs from your innermost heart, from that deepest source. If you recognize that your immediate feelings aren't what you identify with in your deepest self, then it's more honest to bypass them and not act them out. Real honesty is always to act from your heart, from your deepest reality.

AR: I think this is what the behavioral psychologists are trying to do, as best they can—helping clients to act according to their deepest motives. When I was in therapy many years ago, I was wrestling with my inability to criticize others, being unable to say, "Your conduct is inappropriate," in any way. The therapist gave me the assignment of going to a restaurant and ordering a meal and sending it back. It was one of the most difficult things I ever had to do in my life.

BD: And you did it?

AR: I did it.

BD: Under what pretext did you send it back?

AR: That it was no good. "This isn't what I ordered!"

BD: And do you think it really helped you?

AR: Yes. Of course, it was calculated to help me. An arrogant person would never have been given such an assignment.

BD: It seems to me there's a very close parallel here between the psychological approach and the spiritual approach.

AR: Absolutely. Where does psyche stop and spirit begin?

BD: So practice is again, in a sense, acting from the heart.

AR: Two further points occur to me. First, of course, we'll make mistakes, just as a person practicing scales on the piano will make many mistakes. In this sense, the analogy to practicing music is more accurate than the analogy to physical therapy: the main mistake you can make in physical therapy is not doing it, while in music even the most dedicated student is bound to err again and again in various ways. In practicing to overcome shyness, we'll hang back too much one time and be a bit too forward another. Willingness to take risks and make mistakes is necessary; otherwise, we can't possibly learn.

Second, the steps we take in this practice are steps that confirm our sense of intimacy. For example, a teacher standing at the door and welcoming his students will notice intimacy if he smiles when he says good morning. It becomes easier for him to smile because he gets smiles in return. At the beginning, perhaps, if he's ill or irritated, he may not feel like smiling, but if he smiles anyway and gets smiles in return, by the time all the children are in place, he'll have forgotten his troubles.

BD: Such feedback is very important. So is involvement of the whole body. Your example of smiles can be extended to many other things. I read a report of research about people selling tickets, waiting on tables, or doing other sorts of work that brought them into close contact with others. In this study, some of the ticket-sellers, say, were told to brush against the people they were serving, to touch the buyers deliberately but ever so lightly in the course of their interactions. Others were instructed to avoid any contact. Afterward, the people who bought the tickets were asked which of the ticket-sellers were friendly, and statistically, the ones who gave those slight touches were much more likely to be identified as friendly.

Since reading that a number of months ago, I've experimented with it myself. It's remarkable what a strong sense of friendliness and relatedness you can arouse in people, even in very superficial sorts of interactions, by simply brushing against them or ever so lightly touching them. When you say good morning, for example, if you touch them—not necessarily with your body but just with your sleeve—it can make a remarkable difference. A hug may be more than everyone is ready to venture, but surely we can practice warmth and intimacy at this level.

AR: Nobody knows this better than I. It's my tendency to be aloof and cold and stiff, so I consciously try to move that line between the handshake and the hug a bit closer to the hug.

BD: When in doubt, move closer to the hug, to the warmth.

AR: Yes, and as I say, this is difficult for me. Like everybody else, I have a lifetime neurosis, and I need to work on it. Practice, practice.

BD: I suppose this practice consists in finding the source of warmth within you and channeling it in the right direction.

AR: Yes, and taking time.

BD: Giving yourself time? Not being too hard on yourself, you mean?

AR: Taking time in each encounter, giving space to the encounter. Not being in a hurry to move on to the next thing. To stop awhile, in the British sense, meaning to stay. An Englishman will ask a visitor from afar, "How long are you stopping here?" That's what I mean: even if the moment feels awkward, to stay there a while and exchange pleasantries. "How's everything with you?"

The person who is cold and aloof, chances are, would move on at that point—both physically and mentally. When I worked on the staff at the East-West Center, I used to enjoy watching the president of the University of Hawaii circulate through a reception. He had a neat little dance step. He'd be talking with a cluster of people, and at a break in the conversation, he'd step back, pivot toward the next group of people, and take up conversation with them. It sounds awfully artificial, but he really gave his attention to the group he was with, and I think it was sincere attention.

BD: Those are the people we feel are warm—not necessarily the ones who have a warm and melodious tone of voice but the ones who give us the impression that we're really important for them at the moment they're talking with us.

AR: Yes, those who give us attention. Full attention. This is something we learn in formal practice—to devote full attention to the matter at hand, just one thing at a time. One's eye must not be on sequence and continuity but rather on this very thing, the inspiration as it appears. Each inspiration deserves full attention.

BD: Someone may say very friendly words and say them in a very friendly tone of voice, but it's obvious that he or she isn't taking time for you, isn't really present to you or for you. Then we feel he or she had a phony veneer of friendliness.

AR: Look a moment at that word *inspiration*. It means "to take in the spirit." The people who are giving you their attention are taking in the spirit. They're taking in your spirit, making it their own, and thereby enlarging our mutual experience.

PERSONAL BOUNDARIES

BD: Making oneself vulnerable is a very desirable thing, it seems to me, because the alternative is to walk around in a kind of armor that cuts us off and restricts our interaction. I want to be vulnerable, and I appreciate people who make themselves vulnerable. But that's quite a different thing from allowing others to step all over you. The difficulty for me, and I suppose for others, is how to make myself vulnerable yet not allow people to step all over me.

AR: This question strikes home for me. Anne once told me, "You're the only person I ever met who doesn't have a carapace."[1] As you say, that's good in one sense. The negative side is that the slings and arrows of outrageous fortune penetrate pretty deeply sometimes.

BD: I think each of us has a secret that deserves to be protected. In the Christian biblical tradition, it's called the "royal secret of the heart," and I believe in that. When I was in my midteens, a teacher I respected very highly said something to me that was a great eye-opener: "You have to be aware that the temple of the human person has a holy of holies but must also have an inner and an outer court. This has to be built and cultivated in oneself." Certain people are admitted to the outer court, others to the inner court, and very few to the holy of holies. This image stuck in my mind. I realized immediately that it was something I hadn't understood and certainly hadn't put into practice.

AR: The image is very apt. It brings to mind an experience I had recently with one of my students. In my talks, I frequently quote my grandmothers, and this fellow remarked that he thought I was grandmother-ridden. There he slipped into the inner court, and he didn't belong there. He wasn't really where

---

[1] Anne Aitken, Aitken Rōshi's wife. *Carapace:* a hard protective covering (e.g., the shell of a turtle).

he thought he was, and he mistook the configurations of the architecture.

This is one of the real acid tests of practice. When someone treads within our sacred precincts, so to speak, we'll feel genuinely threatened and react defensively—unless we've recognized that essentially there's nothing to protect. All these walls and courtyards are really imaginary. If we've realized the emptiness of the self and integrated it, when someone comes inappropriately close, then we may be able to make light of it—as light as the true nature of the self. But often, at best, this can only be done after the fact.

BD: So the first impulse may be anger or vengefulness, but the first impulse is a reaction, not really a response. You look at that reaction, reject it on the basis of your realization and conviction, then respond in a way that isn't vengeful.

AR: And say a little vow to yourself: this has showed me how protective I am. May I not be so protective in the future.

BD: Fifty years after receiving this lesson about the temple of the heart, I still haven't been very successful in learning it. In dealing with other people, I feel that I know instinctively how much intimacy it's appropriate for me to show, but I find it harder the other way around—getting others to respect the degree of intimacy that feels appropriate to me.

There really *is* such a thing as an appropriate degree of intimacy, don't you think? Why is there such a thing? Where does it come from? Who set it up? I think it's something very different from social convention. There's something else here, isn't there? What is it?

AR: The personal integrity of an individual complements the harmony of all the many beings—of our interbeing, to use Thich Nhat Hanh's word. When we stress one aspect of that interbeing at the expense of another, the dynamics are thrown off.

BD: What would be the two poles?

AR: Harmony and personal integrity. If I'm self-centered, I neglect harmony. If I say it's all one and what's yours is mine, then I neglect personal integrity. Different cultures balance these factors in different ways. For example, in the Samoan culture what's yours is mine and mine is yours to a much greater degree than in our Euro-American culture. So the appropriate, or commonly understood, balance of harmony and personal integrity differs from one culture to another. There's nothing absolute here.

BD: Absolutely nothing absolute? I don't think personal integrity is dependent on culture.

AR: I just mean that in Samoa they put the point of balance at one place along the continuum, and most of us in North America tend to put it at another. Even within a culture, though, individuals put the point of balance at different places.

BD: So where do we take our guidelines from? How can we find a standard?

AR: I think the best we can do is to understand the dynamics of our society. I don't think that we can draw guidelines any more clearly than that.

BD: That indicates that we're dealing here with a very difficult question—all the more difficult in a culture as variegated as ours. Since our society isn't at all uniform, you can't know what degree of intimacy is expected in a relationship.

AR: It's something we're negotiating all the time, something we really have to learn to be sensitive about.

BD: Another question, which also has to do with personal boundaries, is how to say no gracefully. How can we set limits to our availability yet remain generous?

AR: I have a very hard time with this. Not only do I have trouble saying no gracefully, I have trouble saying no at all! So I'm

always getting myself in a pickle, promising to appear somewhere or to write something. Then suddenly the deadline is
upon me, and I have to drop other work in order to fulfill this
commitment. It's a big problem. I try to answer every letter, if
only by scrawling a personal note at the bottom of a photocopied
general letter. Even that takes an inordinate amount of time. If
I allowed myself, I'd be doing nothing but writing letters.

BD: That's the most difficult thing for me also. The brothers
always laugh when I take the mail out of my mailbox. Most of
the other mailboxes are practically empty, and they say to me,
"Do you need a wheelbarrow?" I really haven't found an answer, but perhaps the key to gracefulness in saying no is the
same as it is in dancing—in appreciating the rhythm and flow-
ing with it. There's a rhythm to time, and only so much of it is
available. Perhaps if we attune ourselves to this rhythm, then
we'll be graceful even at a normally awkward moment—when
time is up and we have to cut someone off, for instance.

In many ways, I suppose, saying no gracefully is a problem of
tact. Let's look at tact. What is it, and can it be taught? Is lack
of tact a disability, like being tone-deaf?

AR: Again, surely tact is a matter of being in tune with the
other—of realizing oneself as the other and speaking appropriately, giving him or her the respect we all need in order to grow.
In responding to the actions or comments of others, many of
us have a tendency to use buzzwords: "Don't be careless about
standing up after zazen. Be mindful." In this context, *careless*
and *mindful* are buzzwords. Instead, you could say, "When the
end of the period comes, grasp your knee with one hand and
your ankle with the other, and bring your foot carefully to the
floor." That surely is the tactful and also the accurate way of
giving this reminder. The other way says, in effect, "You're
careless. You aren't mindful." Tact requires avoidance of words
that have become valueless tokens—abstract and pejorative.

BD: Your point about words that have become valueless tokens suggests to me another image. Let's take this hibiscus that's growing here, blossoming and bringing forth tiny leaves, and that little stick on the side there that's dried up. One is alive, the other is dead. That's really the difference between tactful words and tactless ones. In a sense, being rooted in the ground we share is assurance of being tactful.

AR: And the dead stick is the one that hurts.

BD: Right. I also like the musical implication of the word *tact*. In the Benedictine tradition, the practice of listening with the ears of the heart is quite central, and if we cultivate that kind of listening, we'll hear the common tact of the world, which will make us tactful in relationship to others. We'll hear the common music and attune ourselves to it, and so dance gracefully and be graceful. This is what stands behind tact, not mere social convention.

AR: Yes, and I don't think lack of tact is a disability like being tone-deaf. Tact is something one cultivates.

Giving and Receiving Criticism

BD: As we've agreed, no matter how hard and how sincerely we practice, we'll all make mistakes, so it seems to me that one of the most important ways we can help one another is to allow a lot of room for mistakes—to give each other space and help each other be at ease by somehow conveying the idea that we aren't under pressure, that there isn't a right and a wrong way.

AR: Actually, in formal Zen settings such as sesshin, there's a right way and a wrong way to do almost everything, but your point about allowing for mistakes is very important. I tell leaders at the beginning of a sesshin to be particularly careful about correcting others. In the intense environment of sesshin, people often feel very sensitive emotionally, and in the case of newcomers especially, paranoia may lurk right under the surface. So I suggest that leaders allow mistakes to go without correction. If a mistake is repeated and maybe even picked up by others, then a correction is in order, but it's best given as a reminder addressed to the whole group rather than to an individual.

It's also useful to frame a correction in a positive way, saying "Do this" rather than "Don't do that," perhaps not explicitly mentioning the incorrect behavior at all. Just give positive instruction without drawing attention to the error. That way, students figure out their errors for themselves and don't have the feeling of being caught doing something incorrectly.

BD: Praise the positive rather than correcting.

AR: Yes, every parent learns this, I hope. Of course, there's a time when pointed correction is appropriate, too. It depends very largely upon the circumstances and upon the people involved. I remember an instance of this that was instructive to me: when we have a formal meal at the zendo, we conclude by each washing out our eating bowls with hot water or weak tea. After drinking some of the tea water as an offering to ourselves, we pour the rest into an offering vessel. This isn't wastewater in any sense. It's carried away by the servers and later taken outside as an offering.

Anyway, one day after a meal I saw someone casually emptying the offering water over the edge of the porch, and I exclaimed, "What are you *doing*?" That's all that was said. Years later, he recalled this incident, which I had all but forgotten, and said, "That was very helpful to me. It made me think, 'What *am* I doing?' " Afterward, I recalled seeing him many times in the intervening years pouring the offering water carefully on a plant, with his free hand raised in gasshō.

BD: That's beautiful! As you say, whether to give such a correction depends very much on the situation, and even the best teacher or parent probably couldn't figure out what the appropriate response would be; it would take much too long to think it out. If we really are attuned to the situation, however, we'll know when to raise our voices and say something harsh (or seemingly harsh) and when not to. Again, of course, we'll make mistakes.

AR: Indeed. There's also a place for correction of another kind, more along the lines of criticism. I'm thinking, for example, of how Anne has helped me with my writing, particularly in composing the *gāthās* that appear in *The Dragon That Never Sleeps*.[2] When I had a gāthā in a form I thought was pretty good, often she would say, "You haven't got it yet." I'd give it some more work, and in the process, I'd determine better what I really meant. I find gentle challenges are frequently very helpful, particularly when they come from people we're close to.

Over the years, Anne and I have also developed techniques of puncturing one another's balloons—of helping each other see when we're full of hot air, so to speak. We know the game very well now, so it only takes a look or a word to do the trick, to bring the recognition "I'm being rather silly" or "This isn't genuine."

BD: Just by the expression on your face, I can see that humor is the decisive thing here—not taking yourself too seriously.

AR: Yes, we're always on each other's case, but only in a light-hearted way. That lightness is very important, I think. I feel oppressed when I come into homes where confrontation between spouses is the rule, where one spouse takes the other to task in a very serious and discursive way. In our marriage, we're both great teases.

BD: I was just going to ask what you think of teasing.

AR: If it isn't done out of a sense of superiority, teasing has a marvelous role in the family. One needs to be extremely careful

---

[2] *Gāthā:* a brief verse used in practice. *The Dragon That Never Sleeps* (Berkeley: Parallax Press, 1992).

with children, though. Adults shouldn't tease a child except in areas where the child is quite confident and can make the small step of self-recognition that teasing is meant to induce. For example, you can't tease a fourteen-year-old child about a little love affair.

BD: That's very serious for them.

AR: And it's something altogether new and experimental for the child, while it's something old and long-ago for the adult. Most parents can't put themselves in touch with that place of adolescent emotion or can do so only with great difficulty. In such a situation, only the lightest touch of teasing is possible—the most feathery touch, nothing beyond that.

BD: What about teasing in spiritual practice?

AR: I think there's nothing sacred. But again great care must be taken.

BD: I think it's probably safe to generalize that teasing can be a wonderful tool in practice and in relationships but only in areas where a person has achieved a lot of maturity and feels quite secure. Since there are many areas in which we take a long time to mature, great care has to be exercised, even in later life, to recognize when teasing is appropriate. Only very late in life, maybe, is complete teasing possible.

AR: I wonder if we *ever* reach that point.

BD: We've been talking about ways to give correction, but now we're touching on the other side of the question—receiving criticism, whether through teasing or in another way. How can we learn to accept it gracefully?

AR: Criticism that's at least partly true always hurts, and when we feel that pain, that's our chance, our cue to practice. I try to step back and have an honest look at the criticism. Why do I feel pain here? What is it about the criticism that could be true? Sometimes it's a fault that I've thought about before or been called on before, and I can immediately acknowledge, "Yes, you're right. I slipped up." Sometimes it'll be a new kind of suggestion or criticism, and then I'll need some time to reflect on it and to see in what way the criticism is justified. In any case, it's certainly an occasion for practice.

BD: It's not easy for me to accept criticism. I'm so continuously self-critical that if someone else gives me just the tiniest bit of criticism, it can easily be the straw that breaks the camel's back. So if I respond directly in any way when I receive criticism, I usually bungle it, and I've found that the best thing to say is "I'll think about it." That helps me avoid a hasty reaction and gives me time to let it sink in. I think you implied that yourself when you spoke of stepping back to look at the criticism.

AR: With practice, it slowly gets easier to acknowledge our errors. I'm reminded of R. H. Blyth, who used to remark, "I've reached the point in human maturity where I can say, 'What a fool I was three weeks ago!' "

PART THREE

Practicing in Institutions, Practicing in Society

ℵ 13 ℤ

Religious Authority,
Personal Integrity, and
Commitment to Community

BROTHER DAVID: Can you say something about the place of authority in spiritual practice?

AITKEN RŌSHI: Earlier, in discussing the will to power, we spoke of natural authority, a kind of leadership that arises through virtuous actions and is recognized by a community. I think it's important to begin by drawing this distinction between authority that is imposed and authority that is spontaneously given. It's the latter, obviously, that we hope for in religious communities.

The great question we encounter in a society with strongly held democratic ideals is about the place of authority. In every Western sangha that I know, there's a tension between the egalitarian imperative and the need for authority to pass on the teaching. I suspect this tension might be present in Christian communities as well.

BD: Definitely.

AR: Someone once suggested that we have an egalitarian sess-hin, with students taking turns occupying the teacher's place, delivering *teisho* and giving interviews. This was a misguided suggestion, overlooking the need for transference and trust in such a context—a context of deepest inquiry, where self-decep-tion is most likely to enter in. A student might not see the point at the moment for a particular idea or act, but because the teacher presents it, with trust and with transference the student is able to accept it provisionally and allow it to sink in.

Since so much depends on the teacher-student relationship, a student must be very tentative in selecting a teacher. You should poke around, see who's available, see with whom you feel an affinity. I encourage newcomers to take their time in commit-ting themselves to me as a teacher. People may attend any of our events except sesshin, indefinitely, without making a com-mitment to me as a teacher at all. It's fine if they come just for the atmosphere, just to sit with others.

But to move beyond a certain point, a student must decide, "Yes, this is the teacher for me. This is the person for whom I feel a certain transference and trust. I'll go with what he or she says and allow myself to absorb it, to digest it." This isn't an absolute commitment; there's room for a student to bypass what doesn't apply. But it's very important that there be an authority, someone to hold up the mirror and say, "Look! This is what you're doing. This is what you're saying." Or simply to say, "No, that's not right."

The problems come from two directions besides what I've already called the egalitarian imperative. On one hand, some people have old transference still lingering in their minds and psyches, resentments of parents and grandparents, so they have difficulty with a teacher because they're always sticking Daddy's face on the teacher and reacting accordingly. On the other hand, the whole sangha will be poisoned if a teacher betrays his or her own teaching and realization by taking advantage of the trust and transference for selfish reasons.

BD: Everything you said strikes me as relevant and helpful. What I want to add comes less from the experience of being an authority, such as your experience, than from a great, lifelong struggle with the question of authority. Of course, almost everyone wields authority to some degree, so I encourage anybody who feels he or she isn't an authority figure to consider carefully how many people might see them as such. An authority figure isn't just somebody who wears a certain hat or robe. On careful consideration, virtually all of us will see that we do wield authority in one way or another, so I think what I'm going to say is widely applicable.

First of all, I want to ask whether our whole notion of authority today isn't dangerously warped. Looking at a wide variety of English dictionaries, I find that the first meaning of *authority* is something like "power to command." Wielding power over others definitely is one meaning of the word, but if it's become its first meaning, then this says something about our civilization.

The original meaning of *authority* is "that which provides a firm basis for knowing and acting"—very much the way we use the word when we say, "I want to get an authoritative opinion. Should I really have this operation or not?" or when we say, "I really need to consult an authority on this question." It's not a matter of doing but of knowing, not of holding the reins of power but of possessing wisdom. So authority is primarily that which provides a firm basis for knowing and acting; only secondarily does it mean a position of power. It stands to reason that someone who's frequently been found to provide a firm basis for knowing and acting would be given a position of authority. We see this in a village elder or spokesperson or chief, but it also occurs in families. Aunt Emily knows all sorts of good remedies, so when you get sick, you go to her as the family authority on medical matters.

Everything's fine if those in authority positions stay there only as long as they truly provide the firm basis the community needs for knowing and acting. Many Native American tribes set up war chiefs only in times of crisis; as soon as the crisis was over, they returned them to the rank and file. For the same reason, many religious communities nowadays appoint priors and even abbots only for a limited period of time, and then they retire. In the case of my monastery, the abbot is elected for life but with the understanding that every so often he will check if he still has the confidence of the community; if he loses this confidence, he'll step down.

Problems arise when somebody in an authority position doesn't provide a firm basis for knowing and acting but retains the power that was given to him or her (or to his or her predecessors). Power corrupts, as we know, so authority in the historic and sociological sense has a built-in tendency to become authoritarian. That would be my term for a negative authority figure—an authoritarian.

How can one distinguish an authoritarian from a legitimate authority? I've struggled with this for a very long time, but really the answer is obvious once you hit upon it: an authoritarian will put other people down because that's the only way someone who isn't superior at providing a firm basis for knowing and acting can maintain a position of authority—putting everybody else down. To the extent an authority puts you or other people down, he or she is an authoritarian. A true and legitimate authority builds us up. In fact, the words *authority* and *augmentation* both come from the Latin word *augere,* to increase. A true authority augments our knowing, augments our ability to act rightly. It raises you up, makes you stand on your own two feet, increases your power, empowers you.

This may be one of those points where a Christian can point

with a certain amount of gratification to Christian teaching. As recorded in the Gospel according to John, at the Last Supper Jesus gets up from the table and says, "You call me Teacher, and you're right in doing so. Look what I'm going to do now, to show you how a superior and a teacher should act," and then he washes their feet. This is really a historic turning point: it turns the notion of authority upside down. "From now on," Jesus continues, "the greatest among you should be the servant of all." In Christian history, this has by no means always been observed, but at least it's the teaching. From that moment on, what was always true about authority should have been clear— that the only legitimate use of authority is to build up those who are under one's authority.

Everyone's great responsibility in dealing with authority is to question it. Now, the bumper sticker *Question Authority* has a slightly negative connotation, especially in our political situation. I'm talking about a respectful, straightforward, honest question-ing of authority. That's our duty, not just our privilege, because it's what keeps authority on the right track. Anybody who's been in a position of real authority knows how difficult it is to do justice to that position. How grateful we ought to be to any-one who questions our authority and thereby helps us stay on the right track!

AR: So it's the duty of students to make their Zen master a good teacher.

BD: That's right!

LOYALTY VERSUS PERSONAL INTEGRITY

BD: If you have to choose between loyalty to your community and personal integrity, on what basis can you make that choice?

AR: This is a hot potato, isn't it?

BD: It's really a crucial question.

AR: Speaking personally, I can't say I'd have a choice. I can't visualize an occasion when I'd walk away from my own community. It's too much myself. Perhaps that's a fault.

If I speak from observation of others, immediately I find a need to differentiate between two kinds of community—between the immediate community of sangha and a larger net of relationships. Over the years, some people have left the immediate sangha without severing all their ties. Many of them are still contributors, come to the large celebrations, and continue their friendships with people who've remained at the heart of the sangha. We sometimes think of them as peripheral members, but you couldn't say that their loyalty is to the immediate sangha that has its center at the temple. They're not directly engaged in its work of evolution and transformation.

These people have made a choice between personal integrity, as they understood it, as well as they could, and loyalty to the community. They got off the bus, so to speak, but they're still in their own vehicles, driving nearby, heading in more or less the same direction. I respect their decisions and cite this simply as an example of leaving the immediate community yet still remaining friendly with it.

BD: It's very much to your credit as a teacher that they were able to make that move. If I understand it correctly, this is precisely the difference between a healthy spiritual community and a cult: a healthy spiritual community, including the teacher in a very prominent way, will build you up, make you stand on your own two feet, and continuously foster your personal integrity, while a cult will put you down, make you dependent, and erode your personal integrity.

This difference sounds very stark, but in reality, it can be quite subtle. For instance, a community might look like a cult because the teacher has to cater to the students' need for dependence at this stage of their development but intends to wean thm gradually from dependence later on. A new community that has all the signs of being a cult can, at any moment, blossom into a truly spiritual community if that switch takes place—if it really builds up the integrity of the individual members. It's also quite possible that long-established religious communities may, at any time, fall into being cults in the worst sense.

AR: Some of the people who've left our immediate community did feel that they were too dependent and that I and the community generally were making them feel too dependent. In fact, some used pretty strong language, such as *infantilize,* which was rather difficult for me to hear. But I confess that they have a point.

BD: Whether or not they had a point historically isn't important for us and our discussion of practice. What's important in this context is that you and I approve wholeheartedly of the principle that, if a student becomes aware that a community is eroding her or his personal integrity, that's the moment to get out or at least to draw the limits and redefine the relationship with it.

AR: To raise your voice, to begin with.

BD: Of course, the big question is on what basis to take such action.

AR: Exactly. On what basis are you doing it? That's a profound question. In our sangha, one of the reasons given was that I, and the sangha generally, didn't devote enough attention to the needs of parents and children.

BD: I'm not asking for the reasons given. I'm asking about the inner basis of decision making. A cult becomes destructive and maintains itself in this destructive position because the students' inner basis of decision making has been invalidated. The teacher has said or at least conveyed the message that "the only basis on which you can make a valid decision is my command. Do what I tell you. I'm your teacher." How can you regain your independence in such a case? I'm asking in the broadest sense where a person must stand in order to say, "My integrity demands that I reexamine my bonds to this community." Is it simply the shared ground that we call the space beneath the tree?

AR: Certainly, yes. But I think the reason I mentioned—the desire to widen the place of children in the sangha—relates to the point you're making. In one sense, it was the ground for the decision those folks made because it was an essential part of their unfolding as human beings.

BD: It was the concrete and particular form that the space under the tree took in their lives, so to speak, at that time. It was the way the Sacred Heart expressed itself in their lives. But the basic answer is that a choice of this kind must be made on that deepest basis.

AR: From within, I think, it might be expressed like this: "I feel a certain potential within myself. For a while, I felt my potential gradually unfolding in the community, but now I see I can't unfold anymore in these circumstances, so I must move on."

BD: It's ultimately an authority question because, for many people, this kind of question will arise only at the moment when they recognize, maybe for the first time in their lives, that an external authority has authority only because we bestow our personal authority upon that external authority. That's an earth-shaking insight for many people, and there's no way around it: there are many external authorities who make conflicting claims, so the fact that I bow to one authority (and not to another that makes a conflicting claim) can only be explained on the basis of my having recognized a particular authority as truly being authoritative for me.

AR: Even people who continue with a community, as they mature in practice, will experience a shift in their relationship to authority. At the beginning, they're likely to cling to an authority, but later, when they can stand on their own two feet and wield their own sword, they can kill the Buddha and kill Bodhidharma, as it says in *The Gateless Barrier.*

BD: Of course you're not talking about willfulness here.

AR: Certainly not. Willfulness is quite something else.

BD: I think it might be helpful to make a distinction between willfulness and true obedience. Deep listening to your heart of hearts, to the authority within you, is true obedience. Willfulness springs from your private little self, whereas our obedience is to the multicentered self, the interbeing. It's never to your private authority because that ground—that home, that common ground—isn't private.

AR: It's interesting to look at the word *willful.* Full of will. In other words, full of my own will, full of myself.

BD: Yes, full of self-will. I like to make a distinction between one's own will and self-will. The only power that can overcome self-well is one's own will. Our own will is to be built up and made strong. It's our willingness, not our willfulness, that we want to cultivate through practice.

AR: Willingness implies openness.

BD: Yes, it implies openness for interbeing. It implies true listening, listening with our heart of hearts.

BALANCING SOLITUDE AND FRIENDSHIP
WITH THE DEMANDS OF COMMUNITY

BD: Is there a proper balance between solitude and togetherness? As I understand it, community life must have both elements. Solitude is aloneness rooted in community. If it's uprooted from community, then it's not solitude; it's loneliness. Every healthy community offers a certain balance of togetherness and solitude, and each individual then strikes a personal balance within what's possible in that community. If you have a great deal of need for togetherness, you'll still have a certain need for solitude. I suppose it's much the same in families.

The great danger, at least in the monastic setting, is that a person who needs togetherness will infringe on somebody else's solitude, imposing his or her needs selfishly but perhaps justifying it internally with the thought, "Oh, this poor soul is lonely; I'll give him a little company." The opposite situation also occurs: one wants to be alone, somebody else definitely needs companionship, and going off alone is rationalized with the thought, "It's good for her to be alone; she needs the solitude." If we're really living as a community, we should think of one another as responsible in this regard—to protect each other's solitude when necessary and to give the support of togetherness when necessary. I've learned this in monastic life, and again, I think it's probably applicable to family life and to most other communities.

AR: I'm with my wife or with the sangha all the time, from morning to night, so I find delight in taking a trip. When someone drives me to the airport and says, "I'll sit with you till the plane comes," I say, "Oh, no, don't bother. Please leave me, and I'll go along on my own." I treasure that time just sitting unknown in the departure lounge.

BD: I'm completely in accord. The terrible thing is that most of our society seems to have lost an appreciation for solitude. People seem almost incapable of being alone; if they're by themselves, they turn on the TV for company right away. Society today sets a premium on mixing, and the very word *loner* has a quite pejorative sense, suggesting somebody a little cracked, strange, maybe even dangerous. What's to be said for loners?

AR: In Zen Buddhism, we find the term *doku sesshin,* sesshin alone, but few ever try it except unusual people like Sōen Rōshi. He practiced doku sesshin for about two years at Dai Bosatsu Mountain and was thought very strange by his fellow monks. I myself did a doku sesshin for a week once in about 1962 or 1963, camping in a remote place near a Hawaiian village and doing zazen in my tent all day.

In the Buddha's time and in the Buddhist tradition found in southern Asia today, the loner is revered and supported, but in Zen, generally it's felt that sitting alone is denying the fact that we discover in our practice—the fact that the other is myself. Often when sitting alone, one misses the support of others. There's a kind of conspiracy—a con-spiring, a breathing together—that helps us do good zazen. When people write to me and say they're isolated and having difficulty doing zazen on their own, I suggest they sit with the consciousness that they're sitting with everyone and everything in the whole universe.

BD: There's a parallel in the Christian understanding of prayer: there isn't such a thing as private prayer. It's a misnomer. Prayer is never private, because if you put yourself into that place, onto that ground we have in common and from which alone we can pray, you're already in the multicentered self. Privacy makes no sense there at all. Prayer is always communal.

AR: I think loners, at best, embody the multicentered universe and are practicing that. Some people just don't want to do zazen with others; they're natural hermits, happiest when they're alone. Others like to go back and forth, hibernating for a while, so to speak, then coming out, then hibernating again.

BD: I'm concerned that we respect the place of loners in society—in the family, on the job, in religious communities, and so forth. I think their contribution to society is undervalued, and I want to stress that loners, if they're faithful to their calling, are as important to society as mixers. We have to make room, as Thomas Merton said, for idiosyncracies. That was his great appeal to the monks in his own community: make room for idiosyncracies. Don't try to make everybody equal and alike, which is a great danger in our society.

Of course, there are very unhealthy loners in the world, but there are also many very unhealthy mixers. The test is to do either one when it's called for—for loners to mix with others so graciously that no one even notices that they'd prefer to be alone and for mixers to be alone without moping.

AR: Remember, Thoreau had three chairs in his cabin.

BD: In the Christian hermits' tradition, we say that the door of a hermitage must never be locked. Hospitality takes precedence over the hermit's life, if necessary, but those who've chosen the hermit's life have the right to live it.

AR: The question of balancing solitude and togetherness is just one of the issues that arise in the life of a community, be it a monastery or a sangha. Another issue is how to do justice to a special friendship—how to let it flourish without allowing it to become cliquish or exclusive.

BD: Especially in a monastic community, this is a vital task. Within my own time as a monk, there used to be an ironclad rule against special friendships within the community. *Particular friendship* was a technical term. We weren't supposed to have particular friendships and were taught instead to have a loving relationship to the community in general. But love doesn't work in general, so this rule was really a destructive thing. We used to make jokes about it, saying, "Nobody's going to have a particular friendship with you because nobody who's particular would have *you* for a friend." Fortunately, things have changed.

As I see it, the only way a community holds together is if there's friendship all around, in different degrees and different forms—a kind of network of friendships, not some limited type of thing. The intent of the old rule was to prevent a friendship, particularly when it gets strong and intimate, from becoming cliquish or exclusive, as you put it. It has to be understood in the community generally that all friendship is meant to overflow. It's meant to be turned outward, not inward, to be inclusive rather than exclusive.

Now, sometimes there's real suffering in a friendship because the friends can't make it more inclusive. They can't figure out how to include others in certain things because others lack the interest or sensitivity or whatever. In a case like that, this element of pain belongs to the joy of the friendship.

AR: Friendship groups arise very naturally within the Buddhist sangha and can become like little clubs. This can be very destructive, with others feeling left out, like college students who want to belong to a fraternity or a sorority but aren't invited. As you say, there should be a clear understanding that friendships in the sangha overflow into the community as much as possible.

BD: And to the extent this isn't possible, it should be experienced as painful by the friends themselves.

AR: I'm not sure I understand what you mean.

BD: For example, perhaps two friends have a love of poetry. They'd like to share it with others, but they can't because the others aren't interested in poetry.

AR: I see—regret that our friendship in this area can't be shared. How about the friendship that grows up simply out of affinity, without there necessarily being any particular interests involved?

BD: I think there'll always be some interests in common, but imagining a case in which a friendship of mine sprang purely from personal affinity, I think I'd feel all the more, "If only I could have this deep an affinity with everybody!" I think that should be an overtone of the experience. Of course, it's a great gift to experience that deep an affinity with one or two people in a lifetime, and we know it isn't possible to feel such a bond with everyone, but we'd still wish, knowing that everything hangs together with everything, that we could have such love for everybody. That actually seems to be the message we get from falling in love. It's like a flash of lightning that illuminates the scenery and shows us, "This is what it could be like. Everybody ought to love one another this way." For a moment, we see the possibilities.

AR: It seems to me we're touching here on the natural tension between universal harmony and individuality. That kind of individual relationship is in creative tension with universal interbeing, so to speak. My tendency would be to say, "Okay, here's an instance of a particular friendship, and there'll be a certain outflow from that, but it's impossible in the natural order of things for there to be equal love for everyone."

BD: I'd simply add that it also seems to be part of the natural order that, wherever there's love (and there's love everywhere, to different degrees), it always wishes to be shared more widely. In other words, while acknowledging the actual situation, we also acknowledge the ideal that would draw us further toward universal harmony.

ℕ 14 ℤ

The Student and the Teacher

RIGHT RELATIONS WITH A TEACHER

BROTHER DAVID: We've already agreed that it's the duty of students to question a teacher's authority and thus to help make their teachers good teachers. What else is really essential in the commitment a student makes to a teacher?

AITKEN RŌSHI: I think the commitment varies from student to student and from culture to culture. A Japanese monk, for instance, is much more likely than an American Zen student to defer entirely to the teacher.

BD: Practicing unquestioning deference.

AR: Yes. This is very dubious, I think. It's not so much deference as devotion that's necessary if the teacher-student relationship is going to work. You can be devoted to your father and still be angry at him. You can be devoted to your father and talk back to him. But outside the home, you're not going to say anything against him.

BD: Where would you place devotion? We have potential attitudes to the teacher ranging from respect, which is a little cool and distant, to love. It seems to me that devotion is somewhere in between. This is an important subject, so I want to make sure we have exactly the right terminology.

AR: Devotion partakes of both respect and love, it seems to me. For the student, the teacher is an endearing figure. *Rōshi* has become a title, a rather fixed sort of name granted after certain conditions are met, but originally it was a very endearing kind of expression. It just means "the old teacher." Yamada Rōshi restored some of its warmth by sometimes translating it "the old boss." It's a little like the attitude of mixed warmth and respect that the men in our internment camp during World War II took toward R. H. Blyth.[1] They called him "Mr. B." The formality of "Mister" was an indication of the respect they felt for him as an elder, a scholar, and an author, but at the same time, abbreviatng his last name expressed closeness. The name "Mr. B." was quite endearing, and he liked it. He once said to me, "It expresses the kind of love and distance that I really want."

Anyway, this is the kind of attitude I think a student should have toward the teacher—one of respectful love. And this love can bring forth really strong criticism sometimes.

BD: Only if you really love somebody will you criticize that person; otherwise, you don't care enough to take the trouble.

AR: Yes, you're involved in some way.

BD: When you say that devotion partakes both of respect and love, are you saying that there's a little love and a little respect in it, or are you saying that there's a lot of each, as much as possible of each?

AR: I'm not much on respect, to tell you the truth. I accept such formalities as students bowing in the dokusan room and so forth, in part because this is the old custom and in part because I know it's helpful in enabling students to cultivate an openness

---

[1] See the Introduction.

to the teaching. It's not so much to me they're bowing as to the most recent successor of Shākyamuni Buddha, and this may help them throw away the mental and emotional baggage they carry with them.

So I accept this, but I really enjoy being at a party with sangha members and playing with the children there in a way that, I dare say, other teachers wouldn't do. I know one teacher who, when he goes to a sangha party, sits in a room by himself and receives people apart from the rest of the crowd.

BD: I wasn't thinking of external forms of showing respect. I meant the inner reality—"thinking very highly" of someone.

AR: If this isn't earned, it's empty. If I sense a lack of respect from someone, my immediate feeling is that I haven't earned it.

BD: So when you use the term *devotion,* I suppose the essence of devotion would be that the student commits himself or herself to bring toward the teacher—toward the rōshi, in this case—the attitude that he or she'd bring to the most recent successor of Shākyamuni Buddha.

AR: Yes, that's true, as long as it's clear that the teacher isn't asking it for his or her particular personality.

BD: I understand that completely.

AR: Then yes, the teacher-student relationship works best when that devotion is present. Recently, a woman joined our sangha who'd been working for five years in a very traditional setting with a guru. It was imprinted in her psyche that she should worship the guru. I've always emphasized that I'm *not* a guru, a Zen teacher isn't a guru. She projects that on me, nonetheless, and I find that she's able to move along in her practice very readily. I sense it's because she reads me like no student I've ever worked with before.

It reminds me of the case of Clever Hans—a German horse that could do mathematics. He could add and subtract, giving his answer by scuffing the ground with his hoof. When he came to the correct number, he'd stop. He was tested over and over by experts, and they couldn't figure out how he did it unless he actually was performing the mathematical operations. When they took away his trainer and tried it, though, it didn't work. So they brought the trainer back and watched for a long, long time to see if he was signaling Hans. Finally, the experts noticed that the trainer moved almost imperceptibly when Hans reached the right count, and this was the horse's cue to stop.

I think this student reads me in a similar way, taking every inflection of my voice or movement of my eyebrows as a cue. So I must be careful to be completely immobile when I ask her a question. Then she's thrown back on her own resources. This is kind of a variation on the whole theme of right relationship with a teacher. All in all, I think her attitude toward the guru, though not something I'd promote for all students, has been enormously helpful for her practice.

BD: In this right relationship to the teacher, you also include trust, obviously. How about honesty on the part of the student?

AR: Of course, honesty is absolutely essential, not only in teacher-student relations but in zazen itself and in daily life. I tell students, you must be completely honest at the very source of your thoughts. I remember Yasutani Rōshi saying to a student, "If you were completely sincere, you'd be enlightened at this moment." Sincerity and honesty are the very same thing as utmost wisdom. When we're utterly honest, we see things as they are. What more is wisdom that that?

BD: In speaking earlier about the need for students to see who's available before making a commitment to study with a particular teacher, you said that the student should discover with whom they feel an affinity. Could you expand on that a bit? How do you know if you have this affinity?

AR: I remember Sōen Rōshi describing his experience of changing from his initial teacher to the one he finally settled with,

Yamamoto Gempō Rōshi.[2] He said, "When I heard his teisho, I felt something warm here," and he rubbed his belly. Now, not everybody will be able to identify their teachers by a physical reaction like this, but there should be a deep sense of connection, of rightness and certainly of trust.

Affinity is a very mysterious thing, whether it manifests itself in a rare and deep friendship, as we've mentioned, or in the teacher-student relationship. I'd only risk exaggerating the point slightly if I said that our affinities are genetic. I say that to emphasize how unconscious it is. In Japan, *affinity* and *karma* are virtually the same word. The Japanese expression *fushige na en* means either "mysterious affinity" or "mysterious karma." When a couple gets together, they might say, "We must have known each other in a previous life," expressing this feeling of mysterious affinity.

As for how it works in the context of the teacher-student relationship, let me offer the historical example of Ānanda, who was the Buddha's attendant. Though he didn't attain realization during the whole lifetime of the Buddha, Ānanda went on to realize his true nature under Mahākāshyapa, the Buddha's successor, and eventually became the third great teacher in our tradition. Part of the explanation for this is that Ānanda probably was the sort of student Yamada Rōshi called a "person of effort," one whose path is full of obstacles such as self-doubt or jealousy but who practices resolutely and awakens late in life. Another part of it, though, must surely have been an affinity with Makākāshyapa.

BD: This is an important point, it seems to me. As a perfectionist by nature who's often been put in the position of being a teacher, I find this a burning question: do you think there was something in Shākyamuni's psychological makeup that prevented Ānanda from coming to realization?

---

[2] Gempō Rōshi: late master of Ryūtaku Monastery, already in retirement (succeeded by Sōen Rōshi) when Aitken Rōshi studied there in the 1950s.

AR: Yes, but not as a weakness on Shākyamuni's part. It was a complex dynamic with many elements, including Ānanda's readiness, on the one hand, and the quality of affinity between him and his teachers. Affinity and readiness came together in his relationship with Mahākāshyapa, but not in his relationship with Shākyamuni.

BD: In what sense?

AR: The readiness was not mature, and the affinity was not complete. Actually, I've had a similar experience recently, having a longtime student find realization with another teacher.

BD: Is that a painful or a joyful experience?

AR: Oh, it's joyful! I'm really delighted. I have no particular investment in the notion of my personally enlightening somebody.

BD: *You* aren't doing it anyway. The student does it, with the support of all.

AR: That's right, so I'm very pleased about it.

BD: I can imagine the joy of that experience, but I also know that it can be very painful when readiness and affinity aren't complete. A teacher, particularly one with perfectionist tendencies, always asks, "Is that my fault?"

AR: At such moments, I recall what Shunryū Suzuki Rōshi said: "Being a teacher is a matter of coping with one's mistakes."

BD: That's beautiful! We can't improve on that.

GETTING STUCK IN A ROLE

BD: What do you do when your role takes over? I think this can be a serious problem for a teacher or a monk but also for a physician or a mother or a business owner or a secretary.

AR: And for a poet, I would add. I'm thinking of Hopkins again, a very interesting comment he made about writing as a poet—in other words, about writing out of one's role as a poet. Hopkins says Wordsworth is guilty of this, that Wordsworth writes along the path of his own writing. In contrast, says Hopkins, "it is notorious that Shakespeare does not pall, and this is because he uses, I believe, so little Parnassian." *Parnassian* is the term Hopkins uses for overly poetic language. As an example, he quotes Wordsworth's lines "Yet despair / touches me not, though pensive as a bird / Whose vernal cupboards winter hath laid bare," and says this is "beautiful but rather too essentially Wordsworthian."[3] It's too persistently his own poetic way of looking at things.

BD: He's caught in his own role.

AR: Yes, and Hopkins points out clearly that Shakespeare's genius was never to get very caught up in his own role. I think this is instructive for us as teachers and writers and for everybody, really.

BD: In our roles as parents, students, carpenters, photographers, cooks, and so forth, we all need to do the same thing a poet has to do—namely, to approach every situation afresh. What characterizes a good poet is the ability to see with fresh eyes things that everybody else also sees but just checks off as commonplace. Freshness is the decisive thing. We fall into error as soon as we even think, "Oh, I know how to handle *that*" or "I've got *her* number." Every situation is genuinely new.

AR: I gave a talk to children at Green Gulch Zen Center the last time I was there and told them about the time that my father had a stroke and lost the use of his right arm and right leg.[4] When I visited him in the hospital, he asked, "Would you cut my fingernails for me?" I did so and suddenly felt that I

---

[3] Hopkins quotes these verses of Wordsworth as an example of *Castilian,* which he calls "a higher sort of Parnassian."

[4] Green Gulch is a Sōtō Zen practice center and farm near Muir Beach, California, part of the greater San Francisco Zen Center organization.

was the parent and he the child. So I told the children, "You can be parents to your parents, and they can be your children." They were astonished.

I especially remember one eight-year-old girl who couldn't believe it. "How could I be a mother to my mother?" she asked.

I said, "Suppose your mother is sick. You could get a tray in the morning, set a bowl on it, put some cornflakes in the bowl and some milk, then put a spoon and a napkin and a banana beside the bowl, and take it to your mother for her breakfast. Couldn't you do that?" She didn't feel she could, but she was really thinking about it, and I think she got my point.

BD: Of course, once she catches on to this possibility, she'll see thousands of less obvious occasions for mothering her mother, like when her mother is simply tired or sad.

AR: Families that make a game of exchanging roles are truly intimate families. When a child can switch into a nagging role and his mother into a whining role, they can look at themselves and hear themselves and laugh at themselves, and then the argument or whatever problem they were having will immediately evaporate.

BD: That's delightful. It ties into the teasing you spoke of earlier.

AR: Yes, and that's an important point. If teasing is from the inside, so to speak, if you can tease with the child's own voice, then there's no pain, and it's only a joke.

BD: That helps make it obvious that roles are roles and masks are masks—that, deep down, we're all one, playing different roles for the fun of it.

AR: Yes, the mask is the mask, and that's all there is. There's nothing behind it.

BD: How would you help someone, other than children, with this problem of getting stuck in a role?

AR: When I was working at the university, I had a series of secretaries. By way of orientation to the new secretary, I always said, "Look, I know many secretaries do their tasks without question. Their attitude is, 'If this is the way he wants it, this is the way he's going to get it.'" I told them, "I'm not such a person. I don't want you to put out any work you think is wrong. That goes not only for the grammar in a letter but for the content as well. If you think I shouldn't say something I've put in a letter, I want you to tell me." Most of these people had been around longer than I had, and they knew the situation inside and out. So we could be a team. I tried, in this way, to spring them from the secretary role.

It's hard for a subordinate to switch roles with the boss, but I did have one experience at the university where someone else's secretary felt free to speak up and tell me that I'd counseled a student incorrectly. She did it in such a way that I could only acknowledge, "Yes, you're right. I should have been firmer." As I mentioned earlier regarding the episode of sending the food back, my weakness has been an unwillingness to confront or criticize others. What she told me was a great lesson. Maybe not everyone would be willing to listen to it, but I think she knew I would. She might have spoken up anyway, even if she thought I wouldn't.

BD: In other words, to break out of these roles, as a subordinate one has to have the courage to stand up, and as a superior, one has to cultivate openness, a listening attitude, to make it easier for others to speak up.

AR: Yes, if you find yourself in a subordinate position and don't find that space to speak up, if you're confident in yourself, at peace with yourself and if the matter is important, then you can elbow your way in and make the necessary space.

BD: So far we've been speaking mostly about pretty clearly defined family and professional roles. I think this has applications to the subtle roles we play in daily life. For instance, most of us have repetitious ways of interacting with our friends or spouses or relatives. We slide into the grooves of these patterns over and over again: one person makes a sarcastic comment, say, knowing the other will react angrily or make an even more sarcastic response. Maybe there's an argument evolving or just a grim kind of standoff. Anyway, it never gets anywhere. The two people are stuck; they can't find a way to break out of the roles they've adopted with each other.

On a very few occasions, I've succeeded in breaking through role problems of this sort, but only when I prepare myself carefully. First, I must recollect myself long ahead of the meeting, hours ahead, if possible, remembering exactly how the exchange normally goes and where it gets stuck. Then I think of a more creative way of responding to the other person involved and actually rehearse it before going into the situation. When the usual provocation comes, I say something completely unexpected, and all of a sudden, the roles crumble. But this doesn't just happen. You have to be really well prepared and know what you're going to do. It's a little like the comic strip you described—the shy lieutenant who goes to the party and reads from his script: "Hello."

AR: Once again, it comes down to practice. What about breaking out of roles in the context of the teacher-student relationship? I imagine we might have different things to say about this.

BD: I'd be interested to know how you experience this as a teacher of Zen.

AR: I've had experience with it not only from the teacher's side in America and Australia but also from the student's side, working with Japanese teachers. In Asia, Zen students hold to Confucian standards in ordinary situations, rarely challenging the teacher except subtly and obliquely. But in encounters relating to their practice, they're constantly challenging the teacher and other senior people. The precedents for such challenges are ancient, and a teacher encourages them by retelling old Zen stories. In many of these stories, teachers and students switch roles, and sometimes they exchange masks repeatedly, first one issuing a challenge then the other—back and forth, in a kind of dance.

In the United States, some of the Confucian respect for the teacher has carried over, especially where the teacher is of Asian ancestry, but generally it's not strong, and there's not much of it in our sangha. I'm constantly challenged, particularly in the interview room, and I thrive on it.

BD: Of course. A good teacher thrives on challenges, while poor ones find a threat in the merest question. In my novitiate days, I got clobbered more than once simply for asking questions. Sometimes they were perceived as expressing a lack of trust in the teacher, but in reality, I asked precisely because I trusted that the teacher would have an answer or, if he didn't, would search for it with me—which is just as good. All I wanted was to probe more deeply.

Fortunately, most of my teachers didn't disappoint me. After all, a teacher is only an advanced student—and a good teacher knows that and practices accordingly. If we all keep the search, the being "on the way," paramount in our practice, then it's no problem to break out of our teacher and student roles because the roles become secondary and relatively unimportant. That's why Matthew quotes Jesus as saying, "You are not to be called Rabbi, for you have one teacher, and you are all brothers." [Mt. 23:8] That one and only Teacher is the Christ, the true self.

✝ 15 ✝

Sexual Misconduct by
Religious Leaders

AITKEN RŌSHI: Besides examining the general questions of religious authority and teacher-student relationships, we need to confront the specific problem of the abuse of authority, including exploitation of students by teachers and particularly sexual exploitation. This has been a grave problem in Buddhist centers in the United States—Zen centers, Theravada centers, and Tibetan centers—over the past twenty years or so, particularly during the 1980s.

To speak personally, I was appalled at the first instance I became aware of. It happened in our own center, and though the perpetrator wasn't a teacher in a formal sense, he was a monk, and he was our leader. It caught me completely by surprise because my own teachers were not only above this kind of sexual betrayal but also, it seems to me, above any kind of betrayal. I can't think of any real instances where I was let down by any of my four teachers. The teacher-student realtionship is very sensitive, of course, and sometimes I was hurt or maybe even *felt* betrayed, but the supposed betrayal always turned out to be a relatively minor misunderstanding, often a cross-cultural miscommunication.

BROTHER DAVID: In my own monastic life, within the Benedictine tradition, I've spent time in a number of different monasteries and can honestly say that I've never come across an instance of sexual exploitation by a teacher of a student. (In this case, of course, such abuse would be homosexual.) I simply haven't come across it in my thirty years of monastic life, nor have I been told about it. Similar things are certainly going on among Christians: they are as fallible as other humans. But it's largely in places other than the monasteries.

AR: What about the Catholic priest who's out in the world?

BD: I'll have nothing to do with compulsory clerical celibacy. I think it's an abuse of authority and that future generations might well judge our present imposition of celibacy on the clergy more severely than we now judge the burning of witches. The burning of witches was an outrageous crime but didn't have as great a destructive effect on the institution; this insistence on clerical celibacy is destroying the very institution it tries to save.

AR: That's only *clerical* celibacy that you're speaking of, as opposed to monastic celibacy.

BD: Yes, only clerical celibacy. It's a totally different situation than monastic celibacy because priests don't really choose celibacy; they're forced to be celibate in subtle or not-so-subtle ways. This entire issue of sexuality we haven't handled well at all, and I think the time has come when we must do it. Not to do it would be moral bankruptcy.

AR: I think this is also true in the Zen milieu. The teachers who've betrayed their students' trust through sexual misconduct or through serious misconduct in some other realm, it seems to me, haven't personalized their realization enough. They can speak it, perhaps, but that's the easy part. In 1982, when word carried back to Japan about the sexual misconduct of Zen teachers in the United States, Yamada Rōshi said that the kenshō, the realization, of these teachers must not have been deep enough. I want to carry that a step further and say that they haven't *cultivated* their experience enough. They haven't taken the necessary steps to make that experience their own, haven't truly said to themselves, "No matter how lofty the way of the Buddha is, I vow to attain it. I vow in my own way as best I can, to the very best of my ability, to be as noble as the Buddha himself."

BD: Earlier in our conversation, in comparing the Eastern and Western traditions, I suggested that each has its own potential trap. Our Western trap is dualism: the tendency to push distinctions so far that they harden into separations—God, the world, and a gap between the two. I wonder if the problems of misconduct you've mentioned don't occur when someone falls into the corresponding trap in Eastern tradition, the trap of monism: the tendency to melt all distinctions until everything becomes an undifferentiated blur and the feeling arises that anything goes, anything's okay.

AR: I suppose so. That trap has been clearly set forth from the very beginning of Zen work in the West, though. In *The Three Pillars of Zen,* Philip Kapleau called it "the cave of Satan."[1] In Christian terms, it's the antinomian heresy, where a person feels, "I'm saved or I'm enlightened, so I can do no wrong." Perhaps that point hasn't been stressed enough.

I think the sorry record of Buddhist teachers' misconduct in the United States reflects the tradition's Eastern heritage in another way. In North Asia, as I remarked earlier, the Buddhist precepts have been taken very lightly. Now, it would be wrong to generalize here; attitudes in Korea regarding the precept of not misusing sex must be examined as a Korean phenomenon,

---

[1] *Three Pillars of Zen* (Boston: Beacon Press, 1967).

those in Japan as a Japanese phenomenon. I'll leave it to someone else to talk about the Korean case because I don't know enough about it, but I think I have a pretty good sense of the attitudes held in Japan. If you look at the book *Unsui,* which is a humorous but accurate pictorial account of life in a Japanese Zen monastery, you'll find matter-of-fact reference to monks going out on the town.[2]

BD: Climbing over the wall.

AR: Yes, climbing over the wall at night. Where are they going? They're going to the whorehouse, you can be sure. In *Zen Flesh, Zen Bones,* Senzaki recounted the famous story of a monk who regularly went over the wall, using a large stool to get up and over.[3] One night, after the monk had gone out, the abbot removed the stool and bent over there at that same place, so that when the monk returned, he stepped on the abbot's back. You can imagine his horror when he discovered what he'd done! Instead of chastising him, the abbot just said, "It's chilly out. Be careful not to catch a cold," and that monk never went over the wall again.

That's almost like Jesus washing the disciples' feet, isn't it! Unfortunately, it's an unusual case. More generally, there's been a tendency to wink at and ignore such things. As in Christian monasticism, in Zen Buddhism there's been hardly any reference to sex. I've discussed this failing at some length in *The Mind of Clover.*

BD: So now that Zen Buddhism finds itself in a society as oversexed as this one, it will have to develop some way to speak much more explicitly about sex to students and particularly to would-be teachers. A real training in this respect is needed.

---

[2] Giei Sato et al., *Unsui: A Diary of Zen Monastic Life* (Honolulu: University of Hawaii Press, 1973). See drawing 96 there.
[3] Paul Reps, compiler, *Zen Flesh, Zen Bones: A Collection of Zen and Pre-Zen Writings* (Rutland, Vt.: Tuttle, 1957), pp. 101-2.

I've had the privilege of knowing a number of Zen teachers personally, some of them quite intimately, so I've been aware of this problem but never thought, as a friend from a totally different tradition, that it was in any way my role to criticize this misconduct publicly or to get involved beyond helping those who'd gotten injured as best I could. I've watched developments, not exactly from the sidelines, with great interest and hope that the Zen community in America will take serious steps to deal with this dilemma.

The only concrete suggestion I remember making is one that I've now read is being advanced by some lay practitioners of Zen, which is that Zen teachers in the United States (and maybe those in Canada and Mexico or even Europe) get together and set up something like a review board, as we have in other professions. Perhaps it could simply be a board of trusted teachers and alert, long-term students, a board that wouldn't meet regularly but that, in the case of emergency, could be appealed to and would look into the situation. This is a strictly technical suggestion, and I offer it reluctantly, thinking as I do of institutions as necessary evils. Obviously the more important thing is to find a new approach within the teaching and within the practice itself.

AR: I'm afraid a review board would be very difficult to establish and might not work. It could make recommendations until its members were blue in the face, but unless there were some acceptance of its authority, nothing would happen. No, I think we have to look to the sanghas themselves to handle this problem internally. I feel I and others have a certain level of authority respected in the other sanghas, and I've published a number of statements about the problem in general, but I certainly don't want to assume a "holier than thou" posture and haven't felt the authority to intervene in specific situations.

BD: I think that's well advised. You know the famous story in the Gospel of John where a woman caught in adultery is brought to Jesus and he's asked to pronounce judgment on her. The crowd wants to stone her, but he says nothing, giving them a chance to drop the whole thing. When they insist still further, he simply says, "The one among you who is without sin, let that one throw the first stone." [Jn. 8:7] John says, very significantly, that the older people leave the scene before the younger ones. The older one gets, the easier it is to have compassion for people who fall into error. I'm not pointing any fingers.

AR: In my statements on this matter, I acknowledge how difficult it is for me to keep other precepts. As my first Zen friend, R. H. Blyth, once said to me, "When I'm accused of something I didn't do, I bow in acknowledgment of all the things I did do."

BD: Your position and your conduct do give you some authority, but I'd feel uncomfortable for you as a friend if you stepped into any specific situation and tried to exert that authority. It would surely be misunderstood as meddling.

AR: That's exactly what's inhibited me so far. So while I've spoken out on the problem as a whole, I've responded only privately to specific concerns. I feel most of the responsibility to contain misconduct will fall on the sanghas themselves, as I said earlier. The tide of scandals inspired me to propose that our own sangha revise its bylaws to include misconduct as grounds for dismissing the teacher. That's the kind of action I'll be looking for.

THE IMPACT OF SEXUAL MISCONDUCT

BD: Teachers who don't live up to what they preach destroy the confidence of students. Why is this so particularly devastating in the area of sexual relations?

AR: Basically, the sangha is a family. The teacher has an archetypal place in that family as father or mother, and sexual betrayal, seduction of a student by a teacher, amounts to incest.

BD: Rather than assuming that this is understood, I want to pose the question "What is it that's wrong with incest?"

AR: We shouldn't assume *anything* in the area of sexuality, I guess. Peter Rutter, a psychotherapist who's treated a lot of Buddhists affected by sexual misconduct in the various sanghas and who's written a book called *Sex in the Forbidden Zone,* seems to indicate that any kind of sexual relationship between a teacher and a student, even in the academic world, is bad.[4] He says the same about the client-therapist relationship in his own field. Yet many of us know happy marriages that were formed originally from a relationship between a teacher and student in college or psychologist and client. I saw a query in a literature journal, presumably placed by a scholar, inviting people who'd had positive sexual experiences with parents or relatives to tell their stories. I guess there's a possibility, at least theoretically, that such an experience could turn out to be positive.

BD: So this may not be a completely black-and-white matter.

AR: No, but it's safe to say that, in the vast majority of cases, deliberate seduction of a student or someone in an analogous position, taking advantage of the trust that's developed in the milieu of transference, is wrong and tends to be highly destructive. If the person occupying the dominant role feels a serious interest in a certain client or student, before going very far he or she must step out of the dominant role and see to it also that the client or student has come out of the subordinate role and has dispensed with transference.

BD: Not an easy process.

AR: Not an easy process at all—and not the case in the incidents that have blown up U.S. Zen communities. What all the pain and complaint is about is exploitation, sexual and emotional exploitation, of students.

---

[4] *Sex in the Forbidden Zone: Where Men in Power—Therapists, Doctors, Clergy, Teachers, and Others—Betray Women's Trust* (Los Angeles: Jeremy Tarcher, 1989).

BD: That's the decisive word—exploitation. I asked the question about incest to make that point: the thing that makes incest incest is not sexual intimacy between parents and children but the emotional *context* in which the sexual intimacy takes place. From what friends have described to me and what I know as a psychologist, I'm prepared to say that forms of intimacy between children and parents that might appear incestuous to some people may occur not only without damaging children but actually help them. It must be stressed that in these cases the children take the leading role in choosing the kind of intimacy involved.

I would never have brought this up except that you put so much weight on the metaphor of incest in sexual relations between teacher and student. Our society, in my opinion, is extremely warped, both in its appetite for sexual aberration and in its prudery. I don't condone child abuse at all, but neither do I welcome the recent media explosion about it. The self-consciousness that results from it hurts children and adults on a much larger scale than what is labeled child abuse. Do you see what I'm talking about? I'm so disturbed about it because I find hardly anybody who understands this or even has a sense of why it upsets me.

AR: What I think we must recognize in the whole area of sexual relations between relatives, particularly with children, is the very deep-set archetypes that are involved in the roles.

BD: That aspect is, of course, completely respected by the parents I was speaking about—who cultivate a healthy physical closeness with their children. The moment the relationship is used to gratify a sexual urge that a parent feels toward the child, we're talking about child abuse in the real sense—incest and so forth. But our society has become overly sensitive and prudish about physical intimacy between parents and children. Now grandparents are even nervous about visiting their grandchildren because parents or neighbors may interpret any caress as child abuse, and teachers no longer feel they can touch students, even though this occurs routinely in many societies that are far healthier than ours and has a very positive, uplifting effect on the children. Not even the pornography business has done more harm to our society than this frenzy of fear about child abuse. That's my conviction.

AR: Of course, the parents and grandparents who are intimate physically with children are respectful of a certain line that they don't cross.

BD: Absolutely, yes. And I think the reason we need to respect that line becomes clear when we look at sexual intimacy from a different angle: it seems to me that an important psychological function of sexual relations is testing—testing the degree of mutual belonging. When belonging together is unquestionably established on every level, testing it becomes inappropriate. Parents who approach their children sexually betray the children's unquestioning trust in family bonds, which are the prototype of all human belonging, by crudely introducing the element of testing. This testing, which is always present when a parent takes the initiative with a child and which is an integral component of adult sexuality, completely changes the emotional context between parent and child.

This little theory of mine about sex as a test of belonging may help explain why in many societies one has to marry outside the clan or outside the village. It may also shed light on the student-teacher relationship and on celibate communities: it's not that there's anything wrong with sex, just that testing how closely a person belongs to another is totally inappropriate in a context in which mutual belonging is so deeply acknowledged—every bit as deeply, in fact, as in a healthy family.

AR: To get at the archetypes here, let me ask you this: you've spoken of how important it is to be one with the other. In your case, you'd name the other "God."

BD: Very carefully.

AR: In my case, I might not name it. What I hear you saying is that sex is, in its spiritual aspect—and its very real physical aspect, too—the expression of a unity with the other, and a family member is not an other. The father figure in the person of the psychiatrist or the Zen teacher is not an other. Even a sibling is not an other. So when sex occurs in these kinds of relationships, we're tampering with the most profound kind of human patterns.

BD: I think you've interpreted what I said very clearly and succinctly, but you made one small change: I said that the sexual act is a test of belonging, while you said it was an *expression* of belonging. I don't contest that it may also be an expression of belonging, but the aspect of testing is important to me. My argument hinges on the claim that such testing is inappropriate in the kinds of relationship we've mentioned because an unquestionable level of belonging already exists. Belonging may still be celebrated, of course, by expressing it, but without that component of testing, the expression of intimacy (such as the healthy intimacy between parents and children I mentioned a moment ago) isn't sex.

It would be naive, unfortunately, to assume that intense but nonsexual physical intimacy is likely to occur between adults—a teacher and a student, for instance; the dimension of testing would still be present. The only exception that occurs to me is the case of old couples who've reached a time in life when they're so familiar with eath other that testing recedes as an aspect of intimacy. Then their sex life will drastically decline unless their sense of belonging has, meanwhile, grown so deep that the pleasure of expressing their mutual belonging takes over. At that point, sex is transformed into an almost childlike intimacy—a second innocence.

It's interesting in this context to note that testing and expressing are integral to knowing: we come to know things by testing reality, and our knowing is mature when we can express what we know. Of course, *knowing* is the word used in the Bible for sexual intercourse, as when Adam knew Eve, and she conceived.

AR: I think you've taken the matter to its most profound level. Testing and temporarily proving, testing again and temporarily proving—so the process goes, untl a couple reaches that point of maturity in the relationship when the home, the belonging, is truly established. This also accounts for the romantic dramas, such as pretending to be strangers, that some long-married couples cook up, thus creating an imaginary situation in which a test of belonging again makes sense. Obviously, you've given this a great deal of thought.

BD: As a celibate, one *has* to think these things through. Following the normal pattern of society, well, you just follow the pattern, but if you're called in a direction that's quite unusual in your society, such as living in celibacy, you tend to consider what you're doing more carefully.

THE RUSTY-PIPE SYNDROME

BD: I'd like to ask two closely connected questions. The first one has to do with what I call the rusty pipe syndrome. It's not an image I invented but an image that's struck me when, either in a residence or on a city street where a trench has been dug, I see the water pipes that convey our drinking water. Often they look terrible, not only on the outside but also on the inside—very rusty, with all sorts of gunk in them—yet when you turn on the faucet, out comes perfectly clear water that we drink. My question is, to what extent can a teacher who's a rusty pipe in terms of moral conduct still deliver the pure water of the Dharma?

The second question is about students who choose to continue working with a teacher who has engaged in serious misconduct, sexual or otherwise. This isn't a theoretical question; I've spoken with students who sat right next to people injured severely by the teacher, students who could acknowledge this injustice and abuse, even get angry about it, but who would also say, "But I want to stick it out with this teacher. He hasn't done anything wrong to me. I know my boundaries and can stand up for myself, and I get a lot out of his teaching." I've encountered this reaction in a number of instances, not just here and there, among women as well as men.

AR: I've encountered this, too. I think such people haven't taken personally the extraordinary, life-destroying pain that the injured students and their families go through. There've been suicides, you know.

BD: Are you saying that they're not compassionate enough?

AR: It's not so much that they lack compassion as that their compassion is blocked. Their transference is projected with such power and such need that they can overlook or rationalize the pain created by the teacher's misconduct. As for the first part of your question, no, I don't believe the water that comes through a rusty pipe is all that clear or healthful.

BD: That's really the decisive question. I'm certainly not willing to judge a person who stays on with the teacher regardless of his or her conduct. The other question would be important even if no scandals happened at all: to what extent is a teacher's personal behavior, not just in terms of sexuality but in all areas, a criterion for the purity of the teaching she or he conveys?

AR: Well, even at the best, no teacher's behavior is going to appeal to everybody. Every teacher is going to have qualities that turn certain people off.

BD: Sōen Rōshi would be a good example in our time.

AR: I suppose so. The Buddha himself is such an example. We have stories from the old sutras about people who walked away in disgust and despair.

BD: Jesus, certainly, is another example. Plenty of good people walked away from *him*.

AR: Sure. Each person has a set of qualities that affect the affinities we feel. If people don't find affinity with Teacher A, they go to Teacher B. Now, that's for the purest and wisest teacher. As you go down the scale, you find teachers who are less and less pure, less and less wise, until you reach the bottom, where the teachers are corrupt. As you move down this scale, as the pipe gets fouler and fouler, the water is affected more and more, until finally it's poisoned.

BD: This is an important point, so I want to make sure I get it straight. Are you saying that the purity of teaching that a particular teacher hands on to his students is in direct proportion to the integrity of that teacher's life?

AR: I think the two are intimately related, but you need to factor in the teacher's wisdom and insight and depth of experience.

BD: In other words, a highly talented teacher may be able to fudge to a certain extent—to be not quite up to the standards of integrity but still hand on the teaching correctly, truly, and purely.

AR: Yes. I'm thinking of one teacher particularly who, in some ways, is more insightful than I am but has smeared it all over with his corruption.

BD: Thank you. That answer's helpful to me, and I think it might be helpful to many others, too.

❧ 16 ❧

The Imperative to Act

ROUSING THE RELIGIOUS

BROTHER DAVID: In his poem "The Second Coming," a response to World War I and the Black and Tan War in his beloved Ireland, Yeats says despairingly, "The best lack all conviction, while the worst / Are full of passionate intensity." I think he overstates the case, but it's certainly an observable fact that well-intentioned people often lack the passion necessary to meet the world's challenges. They don't stand on their hind legs and take decisive action, while people full of prejudice and greed do that all too readily. Why? I'm at a loss to explain it.

I wonder if this points to an inherent failure in what we teach people who are dedicated and committed to a full Christian life. We help them in their interiority, but we don't emphasize sufficiently that getting involved in the business of the world is absolutely essential to the Christian calling.

AITKEN RŌSHI: I think that's truer of Buddhism than of Christianity. Perhaps the virtues of modesty, perseverance, humility, and so on have been stressed out of proportion. Of course, as I said earlier, in Northern Buddhism the institutions were constantly on notice that they had to conform, and leaders who might otherwise have advocated social involvement naturally kept their voices muted so that only their immediate disciples could hear them. When they were consulted by the civil authorities, they tended to tell the authorities what they wanted to hear. To cite a famous example, Takuan Zenji wrote a letter to a certain samurai, urging him to go into battle with no thought of who was killing, how he was killing, or who was being killed. This was a perversion of the classical Buddhist doctrine that the "three wheels"—the actor, the action, and the thing acted upon—are empty. It omits the blood and the wails of widows and children.

I'm reminded of Jim Douglass's observation in *The Nonviolent Cross* that we can discern two types in the history of religion: the monk in his monastery and the bishop at the cocktail party.[1] Neither of them is involved.

BD: The bishop *thinks* he's involved in politics, and he is to a certain extent.

AR: But the bridges have been built to him; he hasn't built the bridges out. So the interaction occurs on their terms. The poison comes in instead of virtue going out.

BD: This is very much at the core of our whole topic of practice. I think it's one of those areas where something is drastically wrong and in need of reform. Maybe one could put it this way: that it's necessary today to stress that inner achievement has to prove itself through practice and that this includes political action. I think this is true for absolutely everybody. Even the monk sitting in the monastery, the so-called contemplative, can do certain things.

---

[1] James W. Douglass: contemporary Catholic theologian, campaigner for nonviolence, and author of *The Nonviolent Cross: A Theology of Revolution and Peace* (New York: Macmillan, 1968), among other books.

A Zen Buddhist who holds a job with the State Department has different tasks and different leverage than one practicing in a mountain center, but the people in the monastery aren't absolved from political engagement. For a certain period, they may not do anything outwardly, anything one could put one's finger on as overtly political, but they must be deeply conscious of their obligation to the world, and I think even that consciousness itself makes a great difference in the world. After all, political action goes beyond demonstrating and writing letters and making telephone calls to Washington. Turning off the lights and driving at the speed limit . . .

AR: And not paying taxes.

BD: Well, for a monk that's not a problem.

AR: Yes, but if a signficant number of us who do ordinarily pay taxes decided to turn off *that* kind of energy, the government would come to a constitutional crisis, and some sort of correction would have to occur.

BD: Both our traditions, yours and mine, are in a handicapped position in terms of advocating for major change in this society. Zen Buddhism is too new and marginal, still in danger of being branded a cult in the West. We Catholics were marginalized so long that we made extraordinary efforts to be particularly good citizens of the United States. Every church used to have an American flag next to the altar. The profoundly Christian teaching that one should question authority has largely been lost. This is really one of the most basic teachings of Jesus. He says, "On the seat of Moses sit the scribes and the teachers. Do what they tell you, but do not imitate what they are doing." [Mt. 23:2–3] Christians don't act on that.

AR: Except the Catholic Workers and the Quakers and the Church of the Brethren.

BD: Yes, there are some—some of the Jesuits, many of the Maryknollers, and so forth. It hasn't been completely lost, but the difficulty Catholics have in even seeing this need sometimes to act in opposition to civil authority was brought home to me powerfully during the war in Indochina, when Dan Berrigan was in hiding from the FBI. During the many weeks the FBI was looking for him, one of the big networks did a story about him and actually filmed his appearance at a church in Philadelphia to give a sermon. They also interviewed his mother, an aged Minnesota farm woman, as I recall, who had been indoctrinated all her life to be a good Catholic (and an unquestioning citizen). The interviewer asked her first whether her son was a good boy when he was young, and she said yes. Did she know what he was doing now? Yes. "Well," says the interviewer, "it's against the law, isn't it?" The camera studies her face for a long time while she's dealing with this problem. She doesn't say a word, but you see the anguish that is going on, just in her face, in complete silence. After what on television seems an endless time, something like twenty or thirty seconds, she says, "But it isn't *God's* law."

That long pause made it clear how hard it was for her to reach that conclusion and to articulate it. The practice of drawing a distinction between civil law and God's law is not encouraged, not taught. I think it's one of the most important aspects of practice that must be taught nowadays, to Buddhists, you say, and certainly to the great majority of Catholics and other Christians. To return to our question, maybe "the best" lack the passionate intensity of "the worst" because religious formation has failed to instill it.

To Adjust Ourselves or Adjust Society?

BD: How do we find a balance between accepting the world as it is—simply adjusting to what's given—and remaking society, responsibly creating a new society?

AR: This is, again, a tension inherent in human life. You need only to look at the environmental movement to see how some of the clearest thinkers in our culture are struggling with this question. At one pole of the argument are wise people who say to stop monkeying with things, just to let the wilderness alone. At the other pole are equally wise people who argue for various means of stewardship or management that would compromise wilderness, to some degree.

BD: As you say, even great minds are at odds concerning helpful solutions, but I think we can say something concerning helpful attitudes. That's our focus here, in the context of practice. Instead of speaking in terms of the world environment right away, let's talk about getting a new apartment or a new room. What do you do with *that* environment? To what extent do you change it, and to what extent do you adjust to it?

If we bring preconceived notions—"I'm going to change everything. I'm that type" or "I never change anything. I'll just make do with what's there"—the results are likely to be poor, but if you go in and attune yourself to that particular space, it will *tell* you what to do. I think that's an experiential fact. You can go into a room and ask it what it wants from you. It might not tell you in the first ten minutes, but if you spend some time there, eventually it will. If you want to build a house, spend several years on the land before you actually build the house. The environment itself, to the extent that you attune yourself to it, will reveal the appropriate balance between accepting what's there and imposing your ideas on it.

This is true all the more for our world environment. We should encourage people to attune themselves in this way, and we should study the example of others who are better attuned in this way than we are. Our society should take its direction from such people rather than from experts who come with preconceived notions and solutions developed on their drawing boards.

This leads to another question: Given the complexity of life, how can one ever arrive at a clear-cut position?

AR: From an objective point of view, life *is* very complex.

BD: But this kind of question is frequently asked by someone trying to find an alibi, who's not really looking for a clear position but rather is using the complexity of things as an alibi for not taking a position. No political issue can ever be made so unambiguously clear that there's only one position, so someone who's inclined to avoid decisive action will always be able to say, "Well, this is too complex, and there are certainly arguments on the other side." This often has unfortunate results.

AR: Yes, it's apt to make you a conspirator in the general tendency of things to go downhill.

BD: This reluctance to take a position is actually encouraged by politicians of the worst sort, who deliberately try to make us believe that the matters they're debating are too complex for ordinary citizens to understand. "You could never figure it out," they say, "but we have more information, information from experts and even secret information. We're the only ones in a position really to know what's happening." Church hierarchy does the same thing sometimes, unfortunately.

AR: It's a kind of laziness, really, to make this claim that the issues are just too complex. It seems to me that the kind of person who would advance this alibi hasn't cultivated his or her own sense of identity with others, doesn't want to feel the pain of others, and isn't willing to look at the very broadest of the issues involved, where it's clear that this way is right and that way is not right. The very broadest of issues in the Persian Gulf today are that U.S. forces are killing and maiming thousands of people and doing untold ecological damage. In this case, we can't know the details because the news is being censored, but that's enough for me: stop the war.

BD: And not getting involved also is a kind of vote, namely a vote for the status quo. As you say, things change, and if I stay on the sidelines, they'll change in a way that I haven't influenced. Abraham Lincoln said as much: for any disaster to happen, all that's necessary is that enough good people do nothing.

In other words, there really is no way of staying disengaged. It's true that sometimes, despite the best intentions, the results of our actions will not be what we hoped. It's true that, on occasion, our actions may make things worse. But the same can be said for doing nothing. Therefore, we have to take the risk of acting—to examine the issues very carefully, decide what we consider right, and then let the chips fall where they may.

AR: Exactly.

BD: So the complexity of the world is no excuse for indecision or inaction. What if it's not an alibi? What if someone just genuinely has a hard time making decisions? Is there a remedy for indecisiveness?

AR: The Hamlet syndrome! The world is complex, but we tend to make it more complex by allowing the function of our cortex to be complex. When many thoughts press upon us one after another, it's very, very difficult to penetrate them and to see the issues in their true proportions. With practice, we can quiet the mind and increase the likelihood of making a clear and good choice. When the mind is truly at rest, the options will be reduced naturally, and the real choices will loom up before us like great gates. Then you can decide: "I will do this. I won't do that."

BD: Having a sense of the value of time, even a sense of the approach of death, is also useful. Benedictine monks are encouraged to pass death before our eyes daily, not in a morbid way but as a prod to become fully alive. Having a healthy sense of "death as our advisor," as Castaneda puts it, we're likely to become decisive;[2] we don't want to go around and around and around like Eliot's tragicomic figure J. Alfred Prufrock: "time yet for a hundred indecisions, / And for a hundred visions and revisions."[3] There isn't an unlimited amount of time. "If not now, when?"

It's interesting to consider prudence in this light. The connotation given to *prudence* in our everyday language is usually one of timidity and of exaggerated cautiousness. That's really not prudence at all.

AR: No, historically prudence has been very much a virtue. New Englanders used to name their daughters Prudence!

BD: In the scholastic doctrine of virtues, prudence is the first of the cardinal virtues and is likened to a charioteer holding the reins of all the horses that pull the chariot of virtues. It's the mindfulness, you could say, that holds things together and gives each its appropriate place. It's something extremely positive.

AR: Prudence is the middle way between paralysis and abandon.

BD: In a troubled world like ours, how can we avoid cynicism?

AR: Cynicism springs from a very destructive human tendency to reduce and belittle things.

BD: In what sense?

AR: A cynical statement like "The world needs a bloodbath every twenty years" implies that the human being is an inherently contentious, maybe even bloodthirsty animal, destructive almost by nature. I used to hear it in the internment camp from my fellow internees: "It's a dog-eat-dog world." That's the expression of a person who doesn't practice.

BD: That ties in with my own experience. When I noticed cynicism in myself, I looked up the etymology of *cynic*. It's from the

---

[2] Contemporary author Carlos Castaneda quotes this advice from an apparently fictitious Yaqui shaman he calls Don Juan.

[3] See T. S. Eliot, "The Love Song of J. Alfred Prufrock."

Greek work *kynikos,* which literally means "like a dog." That gave me a clue. When I make a cynical remark, it's typically in a situation where I'm confronted with something that demands from me a totally new attitude. Faced with the unfamiliar, I do what a dog does: it barks and snarls at the unknown. Even when I wear something I don't usually wear in the monastery, the dogs are apt to bark at me until they come close and can smell me. If I'm carrying something I'm not normally carrying, they'll bark at this new phenomenon, too.

So here's where it ties in with practice for me. When I hear myself making a cynical remark or find myself tempted to make a cynical remark, I ask myself what's new in this situation that I'm uncomfortable with. I'm up against something new, and it demands a breakthrough, a new way of dealing with the situation. I have to jump to a new and different level. For instance, if I find myself saying something like, "What else do you expect from that kind of a government?" What's demanded from me is an answer to that question. "What else *do* I expect?" The next step is to see if I can do something about it instead of just being cynical. That's practice.

A R : It's so interesting the way this connects cynicism with the trite, overused expression, "It's a dog-eat-dog world."

B D : It's cynical because it doesn't go far enough. If you say, "All right, so what are you going to do to make it not a dog-eat-dog world?" then life opens up again. We're led to a breakthrough that goes beyond cynicism.

A R : This will appeal to those who wish to go beyond, but how do you reach the people who say, "It's impossible. It's just human nature" to be selfish or whatever?

B D : You answered that already when you spoke of practice, because practice is inseparable from the deepest conviction that nothing is impossible, a conviction that in Christianity we call "faith." In the last analysis, cynicism is an angry expression of having set yourself limits that you aren't willing to transcend. The anger is there because, deep down, you know you could transcend them if only you would try.

So cynicism is a dysfunctional sort of attitude. What about the opposite kind of attitude? Does one have the right to be happy-go-lucky in a world like ours?

AR: The night the war in the Persian Gulf began, one of my students remarked, "It seems ironic that I should be so happy and feel so good about myself when the world is going to hell."

I said, "I don't feel very good about *myself*." End of conversation. He called me up early the next morning and asked, "Last night, when you said you didn't feel very good about yourself, did you mean that you didn't feel good about yourself because of the war in the Persian Gulf?"

"You got it," I answered, and he thanked me for this teaching. It's a teaching that goes way back in Buddhism. In the *Vimalakīrti Sutra,* the bodhisattva Mañjushrī asks the archetypal layman Vimalakīrti, "Why are you sick?" Vimalakīrti says, "I am sick because the whole world is sick." Frankly, I lie awake at night and worry about war and other social issues. No, I don't think one has the right to be happy-go-lucky.

BD: "Happy-go-lucky" does suggest a superficial kind of attitude. I agree, one cannot be happy-go-lucky in our world. That's irresponsible. On the other hand, when I look at you and live with you now for a few days, I see a peacefulness that's really a kind of joyfulness. And joyfulness is a kind of happiness that doesn't depend on what happens. It comes from that deepest point of anchorage and is, I think, what we need in our gravely troubled world. Such joy is compatible with feeling very sad about the world or even disgusted with it.

AR: In *The Blue Cliff Record,* there's a kōan in which Yünmen addresses his assembly, saying, "I don't ask you about the fifteenth day of the month."[4] In the lunar calendar of old China,

---

[4] See Thomas and J. C. Cleary, trans., *The Blue Cliff Record,* Vol. I (Boston: Shambhala, 1992). The dialogue quoted is from Case 6.

the fifteenth of the month was the day of the full moon and, as a metaphor, the day of complete fulfillment. "I don't ask you about that day," Yün-men continues. "Come, give me a line about after the fifteenth." Nobody responds, so he answers for the congregation, "Every day is a good day." In so saying, I assure you, he wasn't being happy-go-lucky; he wasn't being a Pollyanna.

Never mind the full-moon days. How about the day when you run over a child with your car? Is that a good day? It's not a good day in any sense except the one Yün-men intends. How do you see him here? In saying "Every day is a good day," he's pointing to something very profound that you just touched on. Can you see what it is?

BD: Somehow that sadness, particularly the sadness of what's going on in our world, gives weight to our joy and makes it worthwhile, which happy-go-luckiness does not. The sadness really belongs to this joy. I'm reminded again of what Leonard Bernstein said about jazz—that he admired it because even the saddest passages have a note of hope and even the most exuberant passages a streak of sadness. There's a balance that keeps us from being sentimental. There's a goodness, a sweetness, even in the worst of days.

❧ 17 ❧

Compassionate Action and the Reshaping of Society

MISSION, SERVICE, AND GENEROSITY

BROTHER DAVID: How do you distinguish between genuine compassion and the "do-gooder" mentality?

AITKEN RŌSHI: To start with, look at the meaning of *compassion*. It means, literally, "suffering with others." So we could distinguish between these two as the difference between working *with* others and working *outside* others for a benefit you suppose they should have. It's a difference between being intimate and manipulative, really. I think of Gandhi going to live among the poorest of the poor, serving them from within, as it were. Of course, there are many examples in Christian tradition of this kind of mission. I think it was my friend Sister Kathleen Reiley who told me the story of a missionary who'd been in Japan forty years and, when he was asked how many converts he'd made in that period, replied quite happily, "Not one." That wasn't his true purpose in going to Japan. Would you say that Christian mission amounts to living compassionately with others?

BD: The two are very closely related, and I like the way you've tied it back again to our deepest experience of oneness and belonging. To the extent that a person has had this experience, she or he will act toward others out of that sense of belonging. She or he will express that belonging as compassion, in the best sense. Some, however, want to do a lot of good for others, but on close inspection, you find that their actions don't come from a deep sense of peace and belonging; rather, they come from exactly the contrary feeling, a feeling of such discomfort with themselves that they have to go meddle in others' lives in order to feel good.

AR: Such people aren't completely in touch with their own pain, in other words; they clearly can't see that the pain of others is their own pain. Again I'm reminded of Vimalakīrti's saying that he's sick because the whole world is sick.

BD: Let me go back, briefly, to your question about mission. Christian mission is a problem for many people, including many Christians, and we could discuss it at great length, but the decisive thing is this: the Christian tradition is essentially missionary because the central message of Jesus is that the kingdom of God has come, is here, is available. Translated into contemporary terms, particularly in the context of our conversation, this means that life according to our deepest experience of belonging is possible here and now, and to the extent to which it is realized, the kingdom of God becomes a reality.

The kingdom of God is, of course, a social reality, not a private thing. The idea that the kingdom of God is within—well, yes, it starts within, but if it stays within, it isn't the kingdom of God. It has to find social expression as a social reality because being human is not a private affair. Being human is a communal affair.

So the missionary, in the full sense, is a witness to the kingdom of God and need not convert people to Christianity. The kingdom of God can and does include people of completely different religious traditions and convictions. It's that human reality out of which all traditions grow and toward which all traditions aim—the peaceable kingdom, if you want, in which not only humans but all creatures of the earth belong together. Many of the cultures to which the missionaries went, though they had some very beautiful and appealing aspects, were fear-ridden cultures, and an essential part of the Christian mission—of establishing that social reality of the kingdom of God—should be to help people overcome their fears. Of course it doesn't help the least bit if missionaries just replace one fear with another, as has frequently happened.

AR: Or replace it with assurances that have no foundation.

BD: "Pie in the sky when you die." Yes, these things have happened. But in all fairness, the job that the Christian mission was meant to do—to alert human beings in the whole world that we're all one family, including the animals and plants, and that there's a way of living without fear—that's surely a positive thing, a liberating thing, that needed to be done.

AR: I wonder about your generalization that fear was so widespread.

BD: You don't think so?

AR: Well, I'm thinking of the other world religions. Surely emancipation is the ideal of Hinduism and Buddhism. . . .

BD: Oh, I was only talking about primal religious traditions.

AR: Shamanism and so on? But even in shamanism, the role of the shaman is to rid you of your demons. Maybe it could be said that Christian mission serves people who've been victimized by the misuse of their own religious traditions.

BD: Yes. Of course, it doesn't help if you bring them a Christianity that's in itself a misuse of the Christian tradition. We're in a very messy situation here.

AR: I just wanted to make a little brief for the native religions.

BD: Well, I think you're right, and I certainly don't want to generalize unfairly, but fear *is* widespread among humans, in our society as well as in others. The key point is that somebody has to dispel that fear. The Christian tradition, like probably all great traditions, has the fearlessness needed to do this because the deep experience to which we keep referring is not only an experience of ultimate belonging but also one of ultimate fearlessness.

Let's go back to our original question or perhaps to a slightly different one: if you discover that you serve others out of a need to be needed, is that a reason to stop serving?

AR: I'd say no, that your discovery has simply thrown light upon your motives and that you can modify your actions accordingly. If you serve others for selfish reasons, then look again, and you'll find deeper motives for serving others.

BD: I'd be inclined to go a step further. If we discover we're doing nice things for other people because we need to be needed, I'd say we should just laugh at ourselves and say, "That's right. I need to be needed. That's one of my needs." Then continue to do nice things, only now being alert to the fact that sometimes you may behave in ways that serve more your need to be needed than others' need for what you're giving. That, of course, gives you the chance to modify your behavior. I think it's very healthy to recognize one's need to be needed.

AR: I agree. If we recognize that we need to be needed, then we may take ourselves a bit less seriously. We can smile when others don't respond. It's okay.

BD: Is there a rule of thumb for balancing concern for "causes" and concern for individual persons? Some of us find it very easy to love humankind and very difficult to love that particular human who crosses our path at this moment and needs help. I might feel enthusiastic about the cause of helping the poor, for instance, and at the same time reluctant to pick up a poor hitchhiker standing beside the road.

AR: In our sangha, it's mostly the other way around: people are quite conscious of immediate needs and rather slow to get involved in causes. I and perhaps one or two others are unduly concerned about causes. The weight of the sangha helps keep me grounded in the more immediate things.

BD: How do you encourage people to look beyond the needs right in front of them, to see and act on the larger problems? How do you help to draw their attention to worldwide issues?

AR: I don't think this can be hurried. It's a gradual process, a matter of personal transformation.

BD: Maybe the trick is to touch those people where they can easily be touched—in other words, with the particular. For quite a while, very few people protested against the war in Vietnam, just the ones who could see the great causes. The great turning point came when, for the first time, on the television screen in their living rooms and in their dens people saw the atrocities of that war.

AR: Yes, so now political and military leaders are careful to prevent the public from seeing such things. We see bloodless feats of technology, maps with arrows, tables of statistics, and lots of press briefings.

BD: The larger point holds, though. There are other ways to bring these great causes home—speaking tours, photographs, personal stories. When friends with means ask my counsel about contributing to causes or to individual needs, I usually encourage them to pick a few causes that they can identify with, or maybe just one. If they become enthusiastic about that, it will help their generosity. I suggest that they also keep an eye open for individuals who need help, cases really limited to one individual—when somebody's car breaks down or something like that. It's helpful in terms of practice to keep a balance between helping a cause, which is a bit abstract, and making a much more direct contribution to an individual as an individual.

THE BIG PROJECT: SOCIAL TRANSFORMATION

BD: People of goodwill are all for universal cooperation, but in practice, it seems to come down to "us" versus "them." Even though we may know deep down that we and our political opponents are one, there remains a realm in which "us" and "them" is simply a given and has to be worked with. How should we approach this contradiction? What attitude shall we hold toward "them" as a matter of practice?

AR: As we agreed in discussing hatred, the key is in learning to love our enemies.

BD: We deal with them as enemies but lovingly. This means that, never forsaking fairness and never denying the humanity of our enemies, we oppose them wherever we can and as far as we feel we must.

AR: As far as we feel we must but stopping shy of violence, right? I'm a pretty firm believer in nonviolence.

BD: That would also be my personal position. Every year, on the first of January, I and some others at the monastery take a vow of nonviolence. At the same time, I have very high respect for some of the people who hold the opinion that violence is acceptable under certain circumstances, particularly in defending the innocent. On an individual level, if a demented person were attacking a child, I think any adult would have a responsibility to defend the child, no matter how deep his or her commitment to nonviolence. Using this as an analogy, an argument can be made for armed revolt against oppressive regimes. I've agonized over this question, especially in regard to situations in Central America, and I can imagine that, if I were there and saw both the need and the possibility of doing something to protect the *campesinos,* I might see it as my responsibility to do something I'd normally reject as a form of violence. This conclusion is completely tentative, but it's the best I can do at this point.

AR: In the same spirit of conjecture, I doubt that I would take up arms for the oppressed; I think my position would be to align myself with the oppressed and to seek some sort of noncombatant yet still supportive role. As I enjoy a good night's sleep and three meals a day here, I certainly am not going to take a holier-than-thou position toward people all around the world who've felt it necessary to fight against dictatorial rulers. I wonder what Gandhi would do. I suppose his position might be to live through the conflict with as much dignity as possible, all the while laying the groundwork for decent social structures after it was over. I can't imagine he would lend energy to killing.

BD: I heard the Dalai Lama address the topic of nonviolence once, and somebody remarked that Buddhists have a good record on war in comparison to other religious traditions. He said, "Well, all religions preach peace, but the followers of all religions have fallen short of this ideal and have waged wars."

AR: Yes, indeed. One frequently hears the glib claim that there's never been a Buddhist war, but as I sit and listen to Buddhist monks from Sri Lanka speak angrily about the Tamils, that notion goes up in smoke. During World War II, Buddhists in Japan temporarily set aside the precept against killing due to the karmic imperatives involved. Even priests were drafted and served on the front lines as combatants.

BD: In the Christian tradition, though the words of the gospel are clear and unequivocal, all sorts of excuses for war-making have been used through the centuries, and many people still go along with this, unfortunately. It's not just that we're being manipulated by our leaders. This is a failure of practice on an enormous scale. We're so susceptible to this us-them thinking. Why?

AR: Looking at human nature from an evolutionary perspective, I think it's true that our id or instinctual life is rooted in the ancient reptilian mind—the primitive part of our brain that developed many eons ago and still is the center for some of our most elementary mental and emotional operations. In more recent times, we've also evolved the capacity to reach awareness of the multicentered nature of the universe. The reptile mind and this other, creative mind—the mind of the universe, you might call it—are in perpetual tension. At times when the reptile mind dominates, we still fall readily into the us-them mode, the fighting mode.

BD: It's not only the reptile mind but also our own human history that affects us. The tribal mind-set—a very strong need to identify ourselves with a particular group and to differentiate ourselves from others—is strongly imprinted on us and easily exploited by war-makers.

AR: That's the reptilian or elementary mind at work in the human psyche.

BD: Research has shown that this mind-set is very, very strong. Somehow it probably has to be acted out. That's about the only way I've found to understand competitive sports: maybe, to a certain extent, they provide a safety valve, allowing this energy to be discharged in a not-too-destructive way.

What about conflict that *isn't* physically violent? Should we avoid it? Should we sometimes be glad for it?

AR: We shouldn't avoid conflict when that would mean suppressing real issues, denying the issues. If there's really a conflict in views, let it come forth. I don't think we should be afraid of interpersonal conflict, but what is the quality of the conflict? What are the terms or means of the conflict? Of course we should avoid yelling at each other. If we keep conflict confined to the issues themselves and learn to practice listening to each other, then conflict can be very healthy.

BD: I would add, avoid conflict in unimportant matters, and postpone it, if feasible, when you're not in a position to deal with it, perhaps because you're sick or it's such a hot issue for you now that you need time to compose yourself and reflect on it.

AR: That's right. And sometimes it's necessary to wait until a skilled mediator can assist you.

BD: Of course, all these positive things we're saying about conflict presuppose that we're dealing with truthful people, people of good faith. Unfortunately, in real life we sometimes are dealing with people who hedge and prevaricate, sometimes people who aren't even *aware* that they're hedging and prevaricating.

AR: Yes, avoid conflict in that situation! I remember Thich Nhat Hanh saying of someone: "I just can't deal with that person."

BD: If Thich Nhat Hanh has someone he can't deal with, that makes me feel a lot better!

AR: Indeed!

BD: You'd think that in a monastery, if anywhere, people would join together with the conviction that they're all after the same thing and want to help one another, yet the degree of personal competition there is sometimes tremendous; the atmosphere can be highly polarized and politicized. In such situations, I've found workshops for the development of discussion-leadership and communication skills truly helpful. They can have a very good effect.

AR: They certainly can, and we can see this development of skills in the sangha or monastic community as part of the long-term process of forging a win-win culture. At least within our own institutions and programs, we can begin to create such a culture.

BD: While agreeing to that in general, I want to suggest that we reserve a small place for the urge to compete and win. Competition may be a necessary and healthy transitional phase for certain people at certain times. For example, adolescent boys may need to go through a competitive period before they can let go of competition or transcend it and find the striving for excellence that isn't dependent on others losing.

AR: Yes, and they may also need a ritual initiation into manhood, as all traditional peoples have. We in present-day Western society have neglected such initiations for both boys and girls, and we may need to restore them in some meaningful way.

BD: Maybe in the context of this initiation one could stress a sense of belonging not just to this tribe or that tribe, this nation or that nation, but rather to the earth and to all the people on earth, the whole human family.

AR: While we're sketching out a program here, I think that we should mention the importance of forming small land trusts and cooperative banks and cooperative farms and stores. All that is quite legal and feasible right now. We don't need to wait and suddenly transform everything. This is the mistake that many reformers have made in the past—trying to create something new out of nothing. The Wobblies had the wise motto "Building the new society within the shell of the old."

BD: Along those lines, I've found enormous inspiration in the work of Hazel Henderson, an economist who teaches at the University of Florida in Gainesville. She's worked out beautifully and carefully some creative ways to transform our economy, even down to such details as establishing local currencies. These are well-thought-out, practical ideas that could eventually be effective in changing the whole of society. The basic principle is always to empower people at the grassroot level—in their shops, neighborhoods, and localities. We've turned over much of our power to the government, and we have to take it back, starting close to home.

AR: Right, and we'll need to practice the perfection of patience, because the process of social transformation is going to be very difficult and very slow and probably very disheartening. Yamada Rōshi expressed the influence of practice on society using the metaphor of adding a chemical to a solution drop by drop: for a long time, nothing seems to be happening, but all of a sudden, with one final drop, the whole solution changes. I don't think we should lose heart because we need to start out small.

BD: No, that's how all great things start. Besides, in reality, this process of social change started long ago. Lots of drops are already in the beaker. We just have to keep our faith strong and add another drop at every opportunity.

Appendix

A Bibliography of Buddhist-Christian Conversations and Studies

Aiken, Charles Francis. *The Dhamma of Gotama Buddha and the Gospel of Jesus Christ: A Critical Inquiry into the Alleged Relations of Buddhism with Primitive Christianity.* Boston: Marlier & Co., 1900.

Altizer, Thomas J. J. *Oriental Mysticism and Biblical Eschatology.* Philadelphia: Westminster Press, 1961.

Amore, Roy C. *Two Masters, One Message: The Lives and Teachings of Gautama and Jesus.* Nashville: Abingdon, 1978.

Appleton, George. *On the Eight-Fold Path: Christian Presence amid Buddhism.* New York: Oxford University Press, 1961.

Baptist, Egerton C. *Nibbāna or the Kingdom?* Columbia, Md.: Gunasena & Co.

Berrigan, Daniel, and Thich Nhat Hanh. *The Raft Is Not the Shore: Conversations toward a Christian-Buddhist Awareness.* Boston: Beacon Press, 1975.

Blyth, R. H. *Buddhist Sermons on Christian Texts.* South San Francisco: Heian International, 1976.

Boyd, James W. *Satan and Mara: Christian and Buddhist Symbols of Evil.* Leiden: E. J. Brill, 1975.

Bruns, J. Edgar. *The Christian Buddhism of St. John: New Insights into the Fourth Gospel.* New York: Paulist Press, 1971.

Buddhadasa, Indapañño. *Christianity and Buddhism*. Bangkok: Nai Buntam Suntornvati, 1967.

Callaway, Tucker N. *Japanese Buddhism and Christianity: A Comparison of the Christian Doctrine of Salvation with That of Some Major Sects of Japanese Buddhism*. Tokyo: Shinkyo Shuppansha Protestant Publishing Co., 1957.

————. *Zen Way, Jesus Way*. Rutland Vt.: Tuttle, 1976.

Carpenter, J. Estlin. *Buddhism and Christianity, A Contrast and Parallel*. New Delhi: Deep & Deep Publications, 1988; also New York: G. H. Doran, 1923.

Carus, Paul. *Buddhism and Its Christian Critics*. Chicago: Open Court Publishing Co., 1905.

The Catholic World. "The Buddhist-Christian Dialogue," Vol. 233, No. 1395 (May–June 1990).

Chang, Lit-sen. *Zen-Existentialism: The Spiritual Decline of the West (A Positive Answer to the Hippies)*. Phillipsburg, N.J.: Presbyterian and Reformed Publishing Co., 1969.

Chappell, David, ed. *Buddhist-Christian Studies*. Honolulu: University of Hawaii Press, 1981–.

Clasper, Paul D. *Eastern Paths and the Christian Way*. Maryknoll, N.Y.: Orbis, 1980.

Cobb, John J., Jr. *Beyond Dialogue: Toward a Mutual Transformation of Christianity and Buddhism*. Philadelphia: Fortress Press, 1982.

———— and Christopher Ives. *The Emptying God: Buddhist-Jewish-Christian Conversations*. Maryknoll, N.Y.: Orbis, 1990.

Corless, Roger, and Paul F. Knotter. *Buddhist Emptiness and Christian Trinity: Essays and Explorations*. New York: Paulist Press, 1990.

Daggy, Robert E., ed. *Encounter: Thomas Merton and D. T. Suzuki*. Monterey, Ky.: Larkspur Press, 1988.

de Kretser, Bryan. *Man in Buddhism and Christianity*. Calcutta: Y.M.C.A. Publishing House, 1954.

De Silva, Lynn A., ed. *Consultation on Buddhist-Christian Encounter*. Columbo, Sri Lanka: Christian Institute of Buddhist Studies, 1963.

————. *The Problem of Self in Buddhism and Christianity*. Columbo, Sri Lanka: The Study for Religion and Society, 1975; also New York: Barnes & Noble, 1979.

————. *Reincarnation in Buddhist and Christian Thought*. Columbo, Sri Lanka: Christian Study Centre, 1968.

————. *Why Believe in God? The Christian Answer in Relation to Buddhism*. Maryknoll, N.Y.: Orbis, 1970.

————. *Why Can't I Save Myself? The Christian Answer to Buddhist Thought*. Columbo, Sri Lanka: Christian Study Centre, 1966.

Dharmasiri, Gunapala. *A Buddhist Critique of the Christian Concept of God*. Columbo, Sri Lanka: Lake House Investments Ltd., 1974; also Antioch, Calif.: Golden Leaves, 1988.

————. *Liberation, Salvation, Self-Realization: A Comparative Study of Hindu, Buddhist, and Christian Ideas*. Madras: University of Madras Press, 1973.

Dumoulin, Heinrich. *Christianity Meets Buddhism*, John C. Maraldo, trans. La Salle, Ill.: Open Court Publishing Co., 1974.

Dunne, Carrin. *Buddha & Jesus: Conversations*. Springfield, Ill.: Templegate, 1975.

Ecumenical Interfaith Relations, Presbyterian Church (U.S.A.). *Christians Learning about Buddhist Neighbors*. Louisville, Ky.: Distribution Management Services.

Edmunds, Albert J., and Anesaki Masaharu. *Buddhist and Christian Gospels*. Tokyo: The Yuhokan Publishing House (American agents: Open Court Publishing Co., Chicago), 1905.

————. *Buddhist Texts Quoted as Scripture by the Gospel of John: A Discovery in the Lower Criticism*. Philadelphia: Brix, 1906.

Eilert, Hakan. *Boundlessness: Studies in Karl Ludwig Reichelt's Missionary Thinking with Special Regard to the Buddhist-Christian Encounter*. Copenhagen: Aros, Eksp., DBK, 1974.

Elenjimittam, Anthony. *Cosmic Ecumenism via Hindu-Buddhist Catholicism: An Autobiography of an Indian Dominican Monk*. Bombay: Aquinas Publications, 1983.

————. *Monasticism: Christian and Hindu-Buddhist*. Bombay: privately published, 1969.

Eusden, John Dykstra. *Zen and Christian: The Journey Between*. New York: Crossroad Publishing Co., 1981.

Fefferman, Stanley, ed. *Awakened Heart: Buddhist-Christian Dialogue in Canada*. Toronto: Canadian Buddhist-Christian Dialogue, 1983.

Fernando, Antony. *Buddhism and Christianity: Their Inner Affinity*. Delhi: Indian Books Centre, 1983.

———— and Leonard Swidler. *Buddhism Made Plain: An Introduction for Christians and Jews*, rev. ed. Maryknoll, N.Y.: Orbis, 1985.

Fingesten, Peter. *East Is East: Hinduism, Buddhism, Christianity, A Comparison*. Philadelphia: Muhlenberg Press, 1956.

Fittipaldi, Silvia. *The Encounter between Roman Catholicism and Zen*. Ann Arbor: University Microfilms International, 1976.

Fox, Douglas A. *Buddhism, Christianity, and the Future of Man.* Philadelphia: Westminster Press, 1972.

Franck, Frederick. *The Supreme Koan: Confessions on a Journey Inward, with Two Buddhist-Christian Miracle Plays.* New York: Crossroad Publishing Co., 1982.

Furlong, Monica. *Zen Effects: The Life of Alan Watts.* Boston: Houghton Mifflin Co., 1986.

Garbe, Richard. *Contributions of Buddhism to Christianity.* Lydia G. Robinson, trans. Chicago: Open Court Publishing Co., 1911.

Geffré, Claude, and Mariasusai Dhavamony. *Buddhism and Christianity.* New York: Seabury Press, 1979.

Goddard, Dwight. *Was Jesus Influenced by Buddhism? A Comparative Study of the Lives and Thoughts of Gautama and Jesus.* Thetford, Vt.: self-published, 1927.

Gordon, Elizabeth Anna. *The Lotus Gospel: Or, Mahayana Buddhism and Its Symbolic Teachings Compared Historically and Geographically with Those of Catholic Christianity.* Tokyo: Waseda University Library, 1911.

Graham, Aelred. *Conversations: Christian and Buddhist, Encounters in Japan.* New York: Harcourt, Brace & World, 1968.

———. *Zen Catholicism: A Suggestion.* New York: Harcourt, Brace & World, 1963.

Grayson, James Huntley. *Early Buddhism and Christianity in Korea: A Study in the Emplantation of Religion.* Leiden: E. J. Brill, 1985.

Habito, Ruben. *Total Liberation: Zen Spirituality and the Social Dimension.* Manila: Zen Center for Oriental Spirituality, 1986.

———. *Healing Breath: Zen Spirituality for a Wounded Earth.* Maryknoll, N.Y.: Orbis, 1993.

Han, Ki-Bun. *Zen and the Bible.* Ann Arbor: University Microfilms International, 1975.

Henry, Patrick G., and Donald Swearer. *For the Sake of the World: The Spirit of Buddhist and Christian Monasticism.* Minneapolis: Fortress Press, 1989.

Houston, G. W., ed. *The Cross and the Lotus: Christianity and Buddhism in Dialogue.* Delhi: Motilal Banarsidass, 1985.

———. *Dharma and Gospel: Two Ways of Seeing.* Delhi: Sri Satguru Publications, 1984.

Ingram, Paul O. *The Modern Buddhist-Christian Dialogue: Two Universalistic Religions in Transformation.* Lewiston: The Edwin Mellen Press, 1988.

————— and Frederick J. Streng, eds. *Buddhist-Christian Dialogue: Mutual Renewal and Transformation.* Honolulu: University of Hawaii Press, 1986.

Irie, Yukio, et al., eds. *A Zen-Christian Pilgrimage: The Fruits of Ten Annual Colloquia in Japan, 1967–1976.* Kyoto: The Zen-Christian Colloquium, 1981.

Johnston, William. *Christian Zen.* New York: Harper & Row, 1971, 1979.

—————. *The Mirror Mind: Zen-Christian Dialogue.* New York: Fordham University Press, 1990.

—————. *The Still Point: Reflections on Zen and Christian Mysticism.* New York: Fordham University Press, 1970, 1982.

Jung, Young-Lee. *Theology of Change: A Christian Concept of God in Eastern Perspective.* Maryknoll, N.Y.: Orbis, 1977.

Kadowaki, J. K. *Zen and the Bible: A Priest's Experience.* New York: Viking Penguin, 1988.

Kang, Kun Ki. *Thomas Merton and Buddhism: A Comparative Study of the Spiritual Thought of Thomas Merton and That of National Teacher Bojo.* Ann Arbor: University Microfilms International, 1979.

Keenan, John P. *The Meaning of Christ: A Mahāyāna Theology.* Maryknoll, N.Y.: Orbis, 1989.

King, Winston L. *Buddhism and Christianity: Some Bridges of Understanding.* Philadelphia: Westminser Press, 1962.

Küng, Hans, and Julia Ching. *Christianity and Chinese Religions.* New York: Doubleday, 1989.

Lassalle, Hugo M. *Zen Meditation for Christians.* La Salle, Ill: Open Court Publishing Co., 1974.

Lee, Chwen Jiuan A., and Thomas G. Hand. *Christianity through Taoist-Buddhist Eyes.* New York: Paulist Press, 1990.

Lefebrue, Leo. *Life Transformed: Meditations on the Christian Scriptures in Light of Buddhist Perspectives.* Chicago: Acta Publications, 1989.

Lillie, Arthur. *Buddhism in Christendom or Jesus, the Essene.* London: Kegan Paul, Trench, Trubner & Co., 1887.

—————. *India in Primitive Christianity.* Delhi: Rare Reprints, 1981.

—————. *The Influence of Buddhism on Primitive Christianity.* New York: Charles Scribner's Son, 1983. "Philosophy at Home" series, Vol. 8.

Ling, Trevor. *Buddha, Marx, and God.* London: Macmillan, 1966.

Lopez, Donald, Jr., and Steve Rockefeller, eds. *The Christ and the Bodhisattva.* Albany, N.Y.: State University of New York Press, 1987.

MacInnes, Elaine. *Teaching Zen to Christians.* Manila: Zen Center for Oriental Spirituality, 1986.

Martinson, Paul Varo. *A Theology of World Religions*. Minneapolis: Augsburg Publishing House, 1987.

Masutani, Fumio. *A Comparative Study of Buddhism and Christianity*. Tokyo: Young East Association, 1957.

May, John D'Arcy. *Meaning, Consensus, and Dialogue in Buddhist-Christian Communication: A Study in the Construction of Meaning*. New York: P. Lang, 1984.

McGuire, Francis J. *Practical Mysticism: The Psychosocial Dynamics of Change in the Mystical Tradition, Christian and Buddhist*, 2 vols. Ann Arbor: University Microfilms International, 1977.

Merton, Thomas. *Zen and the Birds of Appetite*. New York: New Directions, 1968.

Mitchell, Donald W. *Spirituality & Emptiness: The Dynamic of Spiritual Life in Buddhism & Christianity*. New York: Paulist Press, 1991.

Niles, Daniel Thambyrajah. *Buddhism and the Claims of Christ*. Richmond, Va.: John Knox Press, 1987.

O'Connor, Patrick. *Buddhists Find Christ*. Tokyo: Tuttle, 1975.

Pallis, Marco. *A Buddhist Spectrum: Contributions to Buddhist-Christian Dialogue*. New York: Seabury Press, 1980.

Panikkar, Raimundo. *The Silence of God: The Answer of the Buddha*. Maryknoll, N.Y.: Orbis, 1989. Series title: *Faith Meets Faith Series in Interreligious Dialogue*.

Pieris, Aloysius. *Love Meets Wisdom: A Christian Experience of Buddhism*. Maryknoll, N.Y.: Orbis, 1988.

Ratnayaka, Shanta. *Two Ways of Perfection: Buddhist and Christian*. Columbo, Sri Lanka: Lake House Investments Ltd., 1978.

Saunders, Kenneth James. *The Ideals of East and West*. Cambridge, England: The University Press, 1934.

Scott, Archibald. *Buddhism and Christianity: A Parallel and a Contrast*. Port Washington, N.Y.: Kennikat Press, 1971.

Shpakovskii, Anatolii Ignat'evich. *The Reflections of Buddhism in Arthur Schopenhauer, Albert Einstein and Leo Tolstoy: And Its Perspectives in Its Confrontation with Christianity and Marxism*. Huntsville, Ala.: Golden Rule Printing, 1980.

Siegmund, Georg. *Buddhism and Christianity: A Preface to Dialogue*, Mary Frances McCarthy, trans. University, Ala.: University of Alabama Press, 1980.

Smart, Ninian. *Buddhism and the Death of God*. Southampton, England: University of Southampton, 1970.

Society for Buddhist-Christian Studies, Editorial Resources Committee, Harry L. Wells, chairperson. *Resources for Buddhist-Christian Encounter: An Annotated Bibliography.* Wofford Heights, Calif.: Multifaith Resources, 1993.

Spae, Joseph J. *Buddhist-Christian Empathy.* Chicago: Chicago Institute of Theology and Culture, 1980.

Streeter, Burnett Hillman. *The Buddha and the Christ: An Exploration of the Universe and of the Purpose of Human Life.* London: Macmillan, 1932. Series title: Dampton Lectures 1932.

Studies in Formative Spirituality. "A Buddhist Christian Dialogue," Vol. XIV, no. 1 (February 1993). Pittsburgh, Penn.: Institute of Formative Spirituality, Duquesne University.

Suzuki, Daisetz Teitaro. *Mysticism: Christian and Buddhist.* New York: Macmillan, 1957; also Westport, Conn.: Greenwood Press, 1973.

Tambyah, T., and T. Isaac. *A Comparative Study of Hinduism, Buddhism, and Christianity.* Delhi: Indian Book Gallery, 1983.

Thelle, Notto R. *Buddhism and Christianity in Japan: From Conflict to Dialogue, 1854–1899.* Honolulu: University of Hawaii Press, 1987.

Viereck, V. E. *The Lotus and the Word: Key Parallels in the Saddharma-pundarika Sutra and the Gospel according to John.* Cambridge, Mass.: Cambridge Buddhist Association, 1973.

von Glasenapp, Helmuth. *Buddhism and Christianity.* Kandy, Sri Lanka: Buddhist Publication Society, 1963.

Waldenfels, Hans. *Absolute Nothingness: Foundations for a Christian-Buddhist Dialogue,* J. W. Heisig, trans. New York: Paulist Press, 1980.

Walker, Susan, ed. *Speaking of Silence: Christians and Buddhists on the Contemplative Way.* New York: Paulist Press, 1987.

Wells, Kenneth E. *Theravada Buddhism and Protestant Christianity.* Bangkok: Charoen Tham Printing Press, 1963.

Wicksteed, D. James and Anne Saword, eds. *Cistercian Studies,* Vol. IX, Nos. 2 & 3. Proceedings of the Second Asian Monastic Congress: "Christian Monks and Asian Religions," Bangalore, October 14–22, 1973.

Williams, Jay G. *Yeshua Buddha: An Interpretation of New Testament Theology as a Meaningful Myth.* Wheaton, Ill.: Theosophical Publishing House, 1978.

Yagi, Seiichi, and Leonard Swidler. *A Bridge to Buddhist-Christian Dialogue.* New York: Paulist Press, 1988.

Yamaguchi, Minoru. *The Intuition of Zen and Bergson.* Tokyo: Enderle, 1969.

Yoon, Yee-Heum. *A Comparative Study of the Religious Thought of Chi-Tsang and H. Richard Niebuhr: A Comparison and Contrast of the Buddhist and Christian Understanding of Man.* Evanston, Ill., 1979.

Yu, Chai-Shin. *Early Buddhism and Christianity.* Delhi: Motilal Banarsidass, 1981.

Credits

Index